# Weeds in Bloom

Autobiography of an Ordinary Man

# Weeds in Bloom

## Autobiography of an Ordinary Man

# ROBERT NEWTON PECK

RANDOM HOUSE 🏠 NEW YORK

www.randomhouse.com/teens

*Library of Congress Cataloging-in-Publication Data*
Peck, Robert Newton.
Weeds in bloom : autobiography of an ordinary man /
by Robert Newton Peck.
    p.  cm.
ISBN 0-375-82801-X (trade) — ISBN 0-375-82802-8 (pbk.) —
ISBN 0-375-92801-4 (lib. bdg.)
1. Peck, Robert Newton. 2. Peck, Robert Newton—Homes and
haunts—Vermont. 3. Authors, American—20th century—Biography.
4. Peck, Robert Newton—Childhood and youth. 5. Vermont—Social
life and customs.  6. Farm life—Vermont.  I. Title.
PS3566.E254Z478 2005  813'.54—dc22  2004005880

Printed in the United States of America 10 9 8 7 6 5 4 3 2 1
First Edition

# Contents

## Part III: Florida Years

Know a man by those he honors.

# Weeds in Bloom

## Autobiography of an Ordinary Man

# Prologue

My book is your America.

An album of my old friends and your new ones. Real citizens you deserve to greet, and know, and possible remember. You shall know me by the people I have known.

There is no plot.

A happy marriage of Yankee and Confederate, it rambles along Vermont dirt roads and Florida's red clay, meandering like a cow path, seeming at first to go nowhere. But a cow path usual gets to a goal—a freshet of cool water, a barn at milking time, a puddle of shade beneath a meadow elm.

Or a maple.

On the outside, maple trees are rocky hard in their rough tough bark. Yet inside, a sip of springtime sap is sugar sweet. Also in spring, cow manure spread across a pregnant farming field produces a

1

nourishing fragrance. Part of the unseen overture of birth. New life, not yet up. Brown creating green.

Innards differ from hide. That's the mission of my manuscript, to show how plain people can sparkle.

Poverty can etch and furrow the faces of the old or smolder in the eyes of the young. Yet hardship is not always yoked with hardness of the heart. Along with rural innocence, many are graced with charm and backwoods wisdom. Horse sense and cow warmth. They are fresh milk, not from a store but from a stanchion, still bubbling, uncooled and unpasteurized. Raw.

They can decipher the moonlit bugle of a blue-tick hound, dig up cure-all ginseng root, and perhaps steep you a natural remedy for miseries that might plague your body, or cloud your mind.

A few still plant by the star signs.

Others may hunt beneath a possum moon. Or tote around a horse chestnut (a buckeye) in a pocket to prevent an ache. They can skin and gut a rabbit without a knife, and mash wild red choke-cherries for a coughing child. Or snip off part of an implanted porcupine quill to let the gas escape from the shaft in order to reduce its size, and then extract the bloody barb from a newly educated Fido.

Some can locate a bee tree and use the melted comb wax to seal a jar of rhubarb conserve. They drip their own jelly. Their cookstoves, cast only in black, burn nothing but gathered wood to raise biscuits that raise children that raise Cain.

Complaints are rare.

Our American poor are proud of who they are and what crafts they can accomplish (such as fashioning a crude collar for a mule), and will willingly share chow or shelter with a stranger. At times their generosity is a widow's mite, their smiles braving adversity to spit in its eye. After personally digging a grave with their own shovels to bury a loved one, they grieve privately.

Somehow, as uncanny as this may sound to you, country people sense that I came from a humble home and a mix-blood background. Although many are illiterate, they can heal far more often than they can hurt. In a way, for you, I harvest wild herbs of humanity. Some I have known since boyhood. Worthy of gathering.

All, save one, are American, chapters and verses of our nation's past and present. Stars in our flag. Not fancy folk. So please expect no long-stemmed roses from a florist. They are, instead, the unarranged flora that I've handpicked from God's greenery.

Weeds in bloom.

# Part I

# Vermont Boyhood

# Home

"WAIT UP, ROBERT."

My mother's soft voice couldn't catch me. Being seven, I had to be first up the round and rocky slope.

Conquering the summit, I turned to wave triumphantly at Mama, Papa, and Aunt Carrie . . . still climbing. Feet apart, standing astride the treeless top of Lead Hill, I looked far beyond my three family seniors to view our five-acre farm. Below, in the distance, stood mighty Solomon, our ox, with Daisy, our milk cow, black-and-white Holstein specks ankle-deep in silvery crick water, the tassels of their tails flicking the flies of August.

Otherwise motionless, surrendering to a summer Sunday.

From a split between two massive slabs of gray granite atop our minor mountain, juniper bushes

Age seven, in clothes Mama made, with my friend Sambo.

erupted to offer smoke-blue berries. Awaiting my elders, I chewed a few; then, moving a few feet away, found a treat less tarty. Gooseberries. Pale green beads.

Aunt Carrie, a measure leaner than Mama, came to meet me. Then my mother. Papa finished a breathless last.

"Look." I pointed. "Our barn and silo. Smaller'n toys."

Hefting me high to sit on his sinewy shoulders, Papa gripped my knees, then asked, "How's it make you feel, Rob?"

"Biggy. But not big enough. Someday I'm fixing to sprout up into a giant, like you." Sigh. "I honest wonder when that'll be."

"After you finish being a boy."

"When did *you* finish?"

While my legs straddled his neck, my hands felt Papa's face grin. "Never quite did." His head turned to flash a wink at my mother.

Mama smiled. "I hope Rob beats you to it."

From where she stood, Aunt Carrie beckoned to the three of us. "If'n you fetch Robert over this way, he'll see a sight to behold."

Papa deposited me back to ground and we went to learn about whatever my maiden aunt had discovered. Turned out to be early fall flowers. Black-eyed Susans, neighborly to asters: yellowy petals surrounding a button. A brown hubcap, not black. Breaking open a dried center, Aunt Carrie blew away the husks to show me the Susan seeds. Tiny slivers, dark at one end, at the other a dull pewter.

"My," said Papa, "now there's a bunch of boys."

Making a face, I asked, *"Boys?"*

He nodded. "Every seed is a boy. Like you, it probable hankers to stretch at manhood and help to blossom a flower."

Holding one between fingertips, I asked, "Do all seeds actual get to bloom into flowers?"

"No." Papa shook his head. "There's vegetable seed and stallion seed. As you're my son, Robert, you are of *my* seed." He glanced at Mama. "And of your mother's egg."

I blinked. "Like *chickens*?"

My mother smiled. "Right as farming." Then, following a hurried glance at my father, she added, "And that's a plenty on seeding for today."

With a nod, Papa's long arm pointed downhill to our Holsteins. "See there, our dear ol' Daisy knows something we don't." Staring at our cow, I asked what. "Well," my father answered, "there's a clock inside her that notes whenever it's near to milking time. The hour of five."

True enough. Daisy had waded out of the crick water. She headed herself along the narrow brown cow path, dodging through the dandelions and smack toward our barn.

An hour later, Papa and I were there as well. A hickory stanchion with a cotter pin was holding Daisy steady while my father squatted a milking stool. After wiping off her udder bag so that pasture grit wouldn't freckle her milk, Papa began his twice-a-day devotion. Sunday included. A second later I heard the regular cadence of milk spurts chiming into the galvanized metal pail. There was a pure church-bell sound to the ring. Daisy's hot milk blended with her warming animal fragrance, hale and healthy. Like me. While my father milked, Daisy allowed me to reach up and scratch her ears.

Soft brown eyes offered silent thanks.

On workdays, whenever Papa had left our farm to butcher hogs, he'd return wore to bone and more tired than an old boot. Milking on those evenings, my father usual rested his brow on the comforty soft pillow of Daisy's flank.

A plenty more'n once, I had seen Haven Peck do milking with his eyes closed. Possible in prayer. For me, the best prayers have no words.

At bedtime in the loft, my head on rough but clean unbleached muslin, lying on the rustle of a mattress tick stuffed with corn husks, my eyelids were curtaining a long day. Yet prior to sleep, my brain kept digesting what I had been told earlier, away up high on Lead Hill.

About how a life begins.

Papa and Mama had sort of explained how I'd got here. From them. The pair of people who loved me the most: a flower and a chicken. It made me crack a grin.

Someday I'd be more'n a giant.

I'd also be a seed.

# Worshiping My Gods

I WAS A LUCKY KID.

Nearby to our Vermont farm a baseball diamond was paced off, graded level, and marked out. Truckloads of red loam arrived for the infield. The outfield was little more than a pocked pasture of dandelions and daisies, and beyond, a rail fence festooned with poison ivy.

Gods played there.

Nobody like Mr. Tyrus Raymond Cobb of Georgia. Just a rowdy bunch of local guys with little education who toted black lunch pails to grunt jobs, working-day has-beens who became Sunday's heroes. Our hometown baseball team. The Colonials.

Even now, I still remember all of their names, and faces, and the positions they played.

None got paid.

My gods played baseball like a religion. No other reason. They practiced on Friday night, after a day of long sweating hours in wet work shirts. I'm uncertain whether the players wanted us kids to hang around underfoot, staring up at them with our adoring eyes. Yet they tolerated us, protected us, shared their baseball prowess, and gave each one of us a treasure to keep.

A busted bat.

Few of these men ever faked any social polish. They were tougher than the land they lived on, Vermont, and could endure the mills where they labored for a lifetime. Sometimes, following a swing and a miss at batting practice or a bumbled hot grounder, a salty word popped out.

"Hey," another player would remind, "there's kids here."

Such standards ordain ordinary sinners into sanctity. Some of them drank spirits, chewed Red Man tobacco, and did a lot more than merely wink at the women. Yet among them they adhered to a code of righteousness, owing an unspoken duty to the knee-high parishioners in their outdoor chapel. To them, we were cherubs on the ceilings of their souls.

They'd spit on home plate.

Not on us.

These dons of dignity had been knighted by the holy hickory sword of a Louisville Slugger bat, purified by the royal orb of a horsehide sphere. Their armor was flannel; their gauntlets were cowhide gloves, webbed between thumb and forefinger. They were uncut diamonds, worthy of worship, far more precious to me than Tinker or Evers or Chance, the famous double-play trio.

Norm Catlin was our pitcher.

He had freckles on his face and hands, I clearly remember, because Norm had taught me how to grip a curve, a fastball, and a drop. Today it's called a sinker. One time Norm actual gave me a brand-new baseball, virgin white, to keep for my very own. Never had I owned a baseball (except for an old dog-chewed one I'd found), and here it was, all mine.

It slept under my pillow.

Norm was the best player on our team. So good that when he wasn't pitching, he played right field to keep his bat in the lineup. He pitched right and batted left.

Now, whenever Norm Catlin commanded right field, it meant that it was Bick's turn to pitch. He was our left-hander. A southpaw. In a way, I almost loved Bick more than I did Norm, because we all knew that Norm was strong and solid, while our lefty had a sorry flaw.

Bick could handle a baseball, but he could not handle a bottle.

One time, in broad daylight, I saw Bick so drunk that he couldn't stand up. He kept falling. The smell was awful. And there was dried puke staining the front of his good shirt. I ran all the way home and punched my fist through a small glass window in the chicken coop. My hand bled and took sewing. But the hurt of Mama's stitches wasn't the reason I was crying.

Mama and Papa both asked me why I'd on-purpose busted the window. I couldn't tell them the straight of it because I felt too ashamed for Bick, and they final quit asking. Maybe they reasoned that even a kid has a right to a secret.

Bob Klem arrived.

Mr. Klem was a jovial man.

Everyone cheered him, even though he was the in-uniform manager of a visiting team. We all knew that Mr. Klem was well-to-do, as he'd sprung for spanking-fresh uniforms for his entire ball club. He'd made his fortune with a product called Save The Baby, which, I recall, was a bottled syrup that relieved cough, croup, fever, spasm, colic, and other childhood maladies.

If his pitcher threw wild and walked a few of our hitters, we'd see Mr. Bob Klem waddle out to the mound. This was a cue for our crowd to sing the well-known radio jingle:

"Save the baby.
Save the baby."

This always made Mr. Klem smile and wave, as he appreciated the free advertising. By the way, Bob's brother, Bill, was a big-league umpire, well known and respected. Mr. Bill Klem umpired in the National League, starting in the year 1905. He was inducted into the Baseball Hall of Fame in 1953.

Bob Klem had no such big-league aspirations. He just loved baseball enough to be a benevolent manager for a hometown amateur team in the little town of Putnam Landing.

His opposite was Joe Gilbo.

Joe, known in the north country as the Grand Old Man of Baseball, was a dedicated student of the sport. But as manager of the Port Henry team, he never wore a uniform. Just baggy clothes. People said Joe Gilbo was part Indian. (So were a plenty of Pecks.) Several of his sons (and a grandson) played for him.

One of his sons pitched. And if we loaded up the bases during one of our lucky innings at bat, Old Joe would plod slowly out to the pitcher's rubber to confer with his battery (pitcher and catcher). This private conference on the mound always prompted the familiar catcall remark that was hollered, all in fun, by the players in our dugout:

"What'll I do now, Pa?"

There wasn't even a bunt of hostility in this bit of friendly joshing. During the week, our guys and the Gilbo men worked together and were brothers under the horsehide skin.

Sportsmanship existed in the crowd as well as among the players. Believe it or doubt it, whenever a baseball player from either team made an outstanding catch in the field, or belted a homer, our hometown rooters would always applaud his play. Why? Because we respected the game above winning it.

Our team had a unique defensive weapon. We called it our Irish Combination: an able third sacker, Tickle Gunning, and a first baseman, Lefty O'Doole O'Roark. A grounder to third, followed by a crisp in-time peg to first, allowed local rooters to wink at one another, because our Irish Combination had nipped another opposing batsman.

Saturday, to me, was as special as Sunday. Because on Saturday a small pickup truck came to drag our grizzled infield and smooth the dirt for Sunday's game.

Kids, if lucky, got to be weights.

Ballast.

Seated on the husky drag boards overlapped to form a skid, we held on tight, inhaled diamond dust and Ford exhaust fumes, bruised our bottoms, and hooted in rapturous glee. It was dangerous. Hardly the type of excursion a sane mother would condone.

Mr. Ray Catlin (Norm's pa) resided in a tiny shanty close to the ballpark. Its only resident. His job was to chalk the lines. Home to left field. Home to right. He used a one-wheel dispenser over a stretched length of twine.

I helped Mr. Catlin, for free.

In a way, he was a Renaissance man. Owned a big black Belgian plow horse named Dobbin. Could fiddle, and also blow a spirited "Oh, the Moon Shines Tonight on Pretty Red Wing" on a tarnished key-of-D harmonica. Sometimes he'd clog-dance while he wheezed "Turkey in the Straw," get winded, and have to stop to haul in a breather.

All the kids loved him.

As a cook, he seldom bothered with a skillet or a griddle. Instead, Mr. Catlin poured his pancake batter directly onto a hot stove top. He'd wait until each flapjack was riddled with holes before flipping it over. They were so tasty that they needed neither butter nor maple syrup. Just for deviltry, I sometimes teased Mama that even though her pancakes were delicious, they weren't quite the same as Mr. Catlin's.

I'm sure she understood why.

It had to do with baseball and getting coated with diamond dust and Ford fumes, fingernailing a knuckler, trying to tack and tape a broken bat, sleeping with Norm's ball under a muslin pillow stuffed with straw, being hoarse many a Sunday evening in summer, or pretending to knock mud off my cleats (even when I was barefoot). And learning how to spit.

A wise mother rarely tethers an unshod boy whose worst fault is worshiping his earthy August gods.

# Mr. Carliotta

CONSTANTINE WAS HIS FIRST NAME.

However, as I was a little boy and he a mature man with white hair, I called him Mr. Carliotta.

So did everyone. He certainly wasn't the type of senior gentleman that you would greet with a casual "Hey! Hiya, Constantine. How's tricks?"

As a summertime-only resident, he owned a modest white cottage on a pond near our family farm. He arrived around the middle of June, stayed alone all summer, and departed in September, after the Labor Day rush.

He was my boss.

For him, I handled little odd jobs, all of which he kindly designed for a willing youngster: weeding, raking leaves, and generally tidying up outside. I never entered his cottage. Not even once. Only two people did such: Mr. Carliotta, and Mrs.

Filput, who came to clean house on Wednesdays.

We locals all knew Mr. Carliotta was wealthy.

Everybody swore so.

He drove a long, large automobile, and it wasn't a Ford like Dr. Turner's. This was a Cadillac. At the time, during a 1937 rural depression, people who had to travel rode a wagon (usual pulled by a yoke of oxen, mules, or draft horses), a pickup truck, or tractor. Mr. Carliotta's car was the only Cadillac I saw for the first two decades of my life. His auto was big and black. So were his clothes. Black suit, black hat, black shoes. Inside the baggy suit was a white shirt, buttoned all the way up to his neck. Never a tie.

"He's a foreigner," people said. Yet he was a gentleman, and everyone seemed to agree on that.

Our local Italians claimed that he wasn't one of them. No, he wasn't. Mr. Carliotta was originally a Greek. He'd come to America, he told me, as a boy about my age, without a penny and not speaking a word of English.

Now he was a citizen.

Every morning he hoisted our American flag to top a white pole. Often I watched him look upward at the red, white, and blue, removing his hat in reverence. At sunset he hauled the flag down, folded it slowly into a triangle—stars on blue—and toted it inside his cottage.

"To be an American," he told me, "is to feel so far richer than any other person on earth."

"I don't feel so rich."

He shook his head. "Oh, yes you do, Robert, because I sometimes listen as you work, and I can hear you whistle. Or hum. A songbird might be treasured for the same reason."

Sighing, I asked, "How did you get so rich, Mr. Carliotta? I'd like to learn."

"Discipline," he said. As I made a face, he raised his eyebrows. "Robert, do you know what discipline is?"

"Sure do," I told him. "It's when a grown-up makes me do what I don't hanker to. And if I don't do it, I sure get sudden corrected."

Mr. Carliotta nodded. "Well," he said, after a pause for thought, "when you're a child, discipline is directed at you from several sources. Your mother, father, older sisters and brothers, and your teacher. Perhaps even our town lawman, Constable Noe."

"That's right. I catch it from all sides."

Mr. Carliotta pointed a finger at me. "Someday," he said, "you will be a grown man. Then you'll realize that there's only one discipline that counts. It is self-discipline. You'll decide for yourself what you ought to do, because you know it's right."

"But that's not how I'll get rich. Is it?"

After a moment of silence, he said, "Come and

let's walk to the edge of the lake, sit down on that fallen log, and talk."

In a hot rush, I ran barefoot. His big black shoes, beneath the thick cuffs of trousers that always appeared too long, scuffed along over the pebbles, and then stopped. We sat, about seven feet apart.

Selecting a small stone, Mr. Carliotta tossed it into the water. Plop! A ring grew and then melted away, ignoring its cause.

"Robert," he asked, "where is the stone?"

"Gone. It sunk."

"All of it, or just a part?"

"All. The whole thing."

"That," he said, "is what can happen to the money most people earn. It has a way of vanishing. Never to be reclaimed." Not understanding what Mr. Carliotta was explaining, I told him so. "Well," he said, "first let me invite you to throw a stone into our little lake." I picked one up, cocking my arm. "Please do not throw it out into the deep. Instead, drop it very close to the shoreline, into an inch of water. And no more."

This I did.

"In a sense," he said, "we still have it. Close enough to fetch back to possession, anytime we wish."

I agreed.

"You are a polite boy, and you're not afraid of work. So I will tell you my secret. Not really a mystery at all; easy to understand, yet difficult to master." I leaned closer. "A fellow who earns money may often complain that he doesn't earn enough. Because the money is soon spent, and nothing is left. Were his employer to double his wage, or triple it, nothing would be left to save."

"I don't get it."

"His problem, Robert, is not the level of his income. It's the level of his discipline."

"You mean he throws it all away." I pointed at the lake. "Like your stone."

Mr. Carliotta nodded. "The secret is three little words."

"What are they?"

"Always . . . save . . . half."

It was my turn to nod.

"The poor man who only saves pennies will become far richer than the highly paid man who spends every dollar he earns."

"That holds sense."

"Learn," he said, "to deny yourself. People who must *have* a lot of things end up having very little."

I informed Mr. Carliotta that I was saving the loose change he paid me. Already I almost owned a dollar.

"Do you have a bank?"

"Sort of. It's a little tin box that used to have chewing tobacco in it."

"I also started with less than a dollar. As soon as you save five dollars, go to the bank in town and save your money there, where it will grow. It's time you learned the difference between income and capital."

I grinned. "A capital is like Montpelier."

Slapping his knee, Mr. Carliotta smiled at me. "Income is what I pay you. Capital is having that money in the big bank, where it will earn you interest. The bank pays you money to keep it there. And someday, when you are my age, your capital savings will have grown so large that it will pay you all the wages you'll ever need."

I said nothing.

"Income is what you earn. Capital is what you save. And if you deny yourself and wait, you will prosper. Discipline plus patience equals wealth."

"Is that how you did it?"

My first Greek philosopher pointed at my stone, nearby, where it still rested in the shallow shoreline water.

"Robert, it is within your grasp."

# Aunt Ida

SHE LIVED UPROAD.

Aunt Ida had resided in her tiny shack for near about all of her life. No amount of family persuasion could convince her to abandon the place. Or her independence.

From our farm it was most a mile. Uphill.

To visit her I had to hike a double-rutter, as Aunt Ida herself described it, two mules wide. It had been years since the last wagon had ventured up a mountain road fit only for hikers or goats. During the winter set, some of the loggers might use the trail to skid a few logs of rough spruce down to a sawyer, or to the pulp-and-paper mill.

Today I was using it.

As it was August, a winding furrow of fresh ferns had turned the bumpy strip between the wagon ruts a tall green. Amongst the ferns there were weeds, and blue daisies taller than I was, even though my age was coming up eleven. The year was 1938.

It was hot.

Good weather for growing.

To my right, a stand of goldenrod was reaching for the sunshine, fingers extended, like a classroom of young children raising eager hands.

Climbing made the day seem hotter. One of the few summer boilers that stretched field corn, maddened dogs, and could rile up the women in the kitchens who were baking—or worse, canning.

As I hiked, my shirt had become a wash of uphill sweat because of the steep of the pitch. A bug was biting me. Using my free hand, I swatted at it, and possible missed. My other hand toted an unbleached muslin cloth, softer than a Sunday morning due to its countless surrenders to a sudsy brown bar of homemade lye soap in the command of Mama's red knuckles. Inside the napkin rode a dozen baking-powder biscuits, still oven warm, and a small jar of mustard pickles that had been freckled with our homegrown dill.

Gifts for my great-great-aunt. Aunt Ida Peck was reputed to be one hundred and ten years old. Some claimed older.

Alive, but didn't talk anymore.

She really didn't have to. Because near to every-one in the county talked about her, told stories about her adventures, and even whispered about some of her long-gone social activities. Rumor held that a century ago, in 1838, this particular Ida Peck had actual cocked back a musket hammer to full click and, without aiming or sighting along the barrel, shot, wounded, and killed a drunken half-crazed Saint Francis Indian by the name of Three Crows.

At the time, she was only nine.

Others said eight.

All I knew was this: that even now, in spite of Aunt Ida's being well beyond a hundred, nobody ever considered molesting her with as much as a blink of bother. And that included the lowest types you could mention: tax assessors, revenue men, and judges. In her day, all of our Peck clan boasted, Aunt Ida knew how to still the very best whiskey out of sweet corn, water, and maple sugar. One swig would keep a lumberjack warm all winter, up until the middle of May.

A few tongues wagged, remembering a time in her life she'd served in a county jail. Not long, but long enough. A friendly sheriff slid open the bars to her cell and returned her to liberty. This was fair. Because Ida had been imprisoned over a very trivial matter. Nothing serious.

All she'd done was shoot a lawyer.

By that, she earned respect. Even the local

mountain clans, some of which were close to human (others less so)—the Yaws, the Swintons, the Korjacks—allowed that Aunt Ida held her ground. She also was known, and trusted, for holding her tongue whenever she'd been requested to patch up some unlucky buck's gunshot wound. Or stitch a knife gash.

If your prize coonhound poked his fooly nose into a porcupine, Aunt Ida could easy the dog down to quiet and coax out every quill with a pair of pliers. Snip and pull.

She'd shot and skinned the last timber wolf to be spotted in northern Vermont and hung his hide on her front door.

Her only door.

Aunt Ida could needlepoint an entire Bible verse—"Jesus wept"—on a penny button, butcher a hog (tame or wild), dig up cure-all root (ginseng), and for people fixing to sink a well she could locate an underground vein of water by using a divining rod of laurel wood.

Some swore it was willow.

About half a century before I got spawned, General Ulysses S. Grant came hunting in Vermont. It was told to me that Grant personally visited her unpainted house and sipped her special remedy, sassafras tea, supposedly to ease the distress of short temper and long bottles.

There was, however, another reason for General Grant's visit to Vermont: Ida Peck knew horses.

She could walk up to a strange gelding or mare, hold its head, smell its breath, study its eyes and teeth, and then determine if the particular animal was sound or sorry. Closing her eyes, she'd discover a spavin with a few gentle rubs of a hand. General Grant wanted Aunt Ida to help select mounts for the United States Cavalry.

She refused the job, stating that the Civil War had been one awesome mistake, Lincoln's disaster, and little good would ever result from it.

In her time, Aunt Ida never wed herself a husband. Yet she raised eleven children. Three of those children happened to have been her own, born from her body. Several others were stray Pecks, and the remainder had been hatched by shirky and uncaring neighbors. To my mother's knowing, there were forty-three people who claimed her as an aunt, eleven as a mother, and at least fivescore who counted her as a friend. She could drip a pure crabapple jelly as easily as she'd manufacture her own brand of black gunpowder using hearth charcoal, sulfur, and saltpeter. From a few bird feathers Ida could tie trout flies (wet or dry), all of which she could cast and hook a keeper.

Ida Peck knew how to clog-dance, sing over a hundred hymns from memory, recite her own poetry, and quote from almost every chapter in the Scriptures, Old Testament or New.

She could neither read nor write.

But she'd fashion a banjo drumhead from the stretched hide of an ordinary house cat. Needless to say, if the cat was already a dead goner.

So, enough of my bragging.

On with the story.

Before I left our house for uproad that August day, Mama had reminded me that my Aunt Ida Peck was the family matriarch, an ancient who warranted my very best company manners. She was also the oldest living Peck in all of Vermont, my mother told me while she added a lick or two of pomade to sweeten my hair and mask my farm-boy fragrance.

Ready to pay call, I arrived.

The old woman was barefoot. With her eyes closed and mouth open, she rested in her rocker chair on the almost grassless dirt by her door. Her complexion was paler than a flour sack.

"Aunt Ida," I called softly.

It took repeating.

Opening her eyes, she stared at a summer sky, then finally looked my way, as though questioning who I was. Foe or friend? A lad of ten winters or General Ulysses S. Grant?

"It's me," I told her. "Robert. My father is Haven

Peck, the third son of my grandfather Newton Peck." I paused for a breath. "You are my great-great-aunt."

Slowly her mouth closed, and for one forever-to-be-cherished moment, the flag blue returned to her eyes, studying me, possible wondering whether I'd ever measure up to manhood, to being a Peck and her kin.

I stayed for over an hour, listening to bluebirds and reading her a poem I'd composed. It was the last time I saw her alive.

I'm now over seventy. So sixty years later, I am still asking myself if I am worthy enough to call her . . . my Aunt Ida.

# Mr. Diskin

BARNEY DISKIN WAS A JEW.

Everybody in the entire town knew it, so there wasn't any hope for Mr. Diskin to fib, claiming he wasn't when he righteous was.

"Give him credit," Papa said. "He ain't ashamed of it."

"No," said Mama. "He walks with his head up high, just as though he was a normal everyday Vermonter."

"A mite uppity," said my Aunt Carrie, "seeing as he's nothing more than a junk dealer."

Even before my weaning (or shortly thereafter), I had been informed that old Barney Diskin was Jewish, though beyond my toddling years I had little or no idea exactly what a Jew really was. Nor did I bother a fig. No sleep lost. Jews, in the northern mountains of Vermont, were about as prevalent as laughter in church, or folding money in a collection plate.

In our town there was only one.

Mr. Barney Diskin.

Nobody seemed to care ample much. Several of the members of the Election Board swore up and down that Mr. Diskin always voted straight Republican, even as far back as Theodore Roosevelt. Such historical authenticity was good enough for an Ivory-soap percentage of the local citizenry. It proved, beyond any doubt, that Barney Diskin was maybe a Jew, but definitely not one of those city types who appeared every summer along with the gnats.

Besides, he wasn't a dang renter. Or a tourist. Mr. Diskin owned his land in fee simple absolute.

In Vermont, land is solid. Therefore, whenever folks possessed it and paid the taxes that fell due, this was prima facie evidence that they were burghers who rightly commanded Green Mountain State *turf,* resolute as the statue of the granite sentry that collected pigeon drop on our village square.

We all, somehow, grew to be as proud of our only Jew as we were of our only statue.

Solid was solid.

Prouder, in fact, of Mr. Diskin. For good reason. Our granite Minute Man never coughed up even a mill of tax loot. Barney Diskin did. So Vermonters, being as they customarily were (tighter than a bull's butt in fly time), long ago concluded that Mr. Diskin was a Republican, a paid-up citizen in good standing, and a worthy neighbor.

Even though nobody in New England ever took such a bold step as to throw something away, every town needed a junk depository. And, therefore, a junk dealer.

If you couldn't lug (schlep) your junky stuff to Barney's Junk, his wagon would, eventual, come to you to collect it in person . . . and help you pile it aboard.

There was talk.

Not about Mr. Barney Diskin.

But concerning his mule.

Veronica, everybody in town had observed, was skinny. This, for some strange reason, caused tongues to wag. Gossipers insisted that Veronica's lean condition was due to her lack of proper nourishment—in turn, a result of the indisputable fact that Mr. Barney Diskin was too much of a skin-flint to afford her ample hay or oatage.

Mr. Diskin was criticized even by Miss Maudie Rickford, whose canary had died of malnutrition.

People who knew nothing of hay, oats, or even sorghum expressed their opinions of what they now considered to be a proper mule's diet. Had faithful old Veronica been owned by a Yankee (or even an Irisher or a Eye-talian), little or no concern would have seeped through the clapboards and into the ether of local public opinion.

But dear Veronica, it seemed, was hardly an ordinary mule.

She became . . . "that Jew's mule."

Families who had starved, beaten, and neglected their livestock for no less than seven generations were up in arms. A local S.P.C.A. was formed. A Society for the Prevention of Cruelty to Animals. Three people (two of whom were beyond the sprightly age of eighty) attended the first meeting.

Both of the octogenarians, who presumed that the assembly didn't revolve around mule treatment but hoped it was about embroidery, fell asleep before the call to order. Nonetheless, their mere presence was computed to mean that all locals were socially aware of the eroding standards of animal husbandry now rampantly raging in our otherwise pro-bees/birds/beasties community.

It was almost as if someone had neglected Rin Tin Tin or Lassie.

A local veterinarian, however, stemmed a tidal wave of hysteria by conducting a complete examination of Veronica and concluding that (like people) some mules are chunky. Others are rails.

And there was absolutely no justification for either a citizen's arrest or a search and seizure.

Mr. Diskin's next-door neighbor, Miss Elspeth Hardigan, testified that for years she had observed her friend Barney tending and grooming and curry-combing his mule. No animal since the elephants of Hannibal had received such devoted benevolence, according to Miss Hardigan's deposition.

The local S.P.C.A. then disbanded. Two of its three members had passed away. Their sudden demise wasn't at all due to Mr. Diskin's innocence, but rather to the unexpected levy of membership dues.

Veronica, the town decided, just happened to be a skinny mule, one of the eccentricities of nature, an accepted phenomenon.

Through it all, Veronica, though she had been the nucleus of attention, remained impervious to the publicity and maintained her usual I-don't-give-a-haw nonchalance, in which she had established more than a modicum of equity.

Soup Vinson (his righteous name was Luther Wesley Vinson; he was over a year my senior and also my next-farm neighbor) and I called regularly at Mr. Diskin's place.

Our calls were not social.

They were business.

Hearing from several of the more mature entrepreneurs—those in the sixth grade—that a kid could collect tinfoil and sell it, we became instant collectors.

And bankers.

Our bank was burglarproof, consisting of a rusty tomato can, a cylindrical vault that had earlier been used for fishing worms. Without as much as a wash or rinse, Soup and I completed its conversion from a holder of warm bait to one of cold cash.

After several false starts (the most useless being when we mistook lead foil for tinfoil), our shining ball began slowly to grow, nourished mainly by inner sleeves of chewing gum.

Then we hit the jackpot.

Dolores Baginski's Beauty Salon.

Braving its odor, a fragrance far worse than the dump's or that of the alley behind Filput's Fish, we rummaged through the trash cans at the beauty parlor in search of that treasure of all treasures, a discarded Kinky-Perm curler wrap. This prize, our expertise informed us, wasn't lead. This shiny stuff was what Mr. Diskin would buy—the real McCoy, a metallic mother lode.

Tin.

At three o'clock after school each day, Soup Vinson and I made a frontal attack on Mrs. Baginski's rear. We found, collected, and finally sold.

For cash.

Business was a boom.

At almost any given time our tomato-can bank, buried beneath old Mr. Dilworth Cooperston's outhouse, held a trove of anywhere between eight cents all the way up to a staggering total of twenty-two.

At first, the spheres of tinfoil that we hauled to the junk dealer, usual at a full gallop, boasted a diameter of one inch.

Even though Mr. Diskin sighed or smiled, he coughed up a penny. He pointed at our foil ball, slightly larger than a prayer bead, and shook his head. Then, pointing to a ball of tinfoil bigger than a prize county-fair cabbage, he nodded. Mr. Diskin never spoke. He wasn't one to waste words, even when Soup and I were wasting his time, and ours.

From that day forward, however, we only presented our tinfoil to Mr. Diskin on Saturday. For good reason. Saturday afternoon, for kids who could afford a ten-cent ticket, was movie day. A matinee double feature starring that fabulous world adventurer, Fearless Ferguson, plus a western with big-name singing cowboys such as Hoot Holler or Buffalo Trill.

On Saturday mornings, Mr. Diskin made sure that every youngster got ten cents because he knew why it was necessary. I remember all those shiny new dimes, always ready for deposit into our movie-anticipating hands.

"Papa," I asked my father, "how come old Mr. Diskin doesn't ever say anything? Can't he talk at all? Seems to me Mr. Diskin ought to dicker with us, you know, on the price of what we're bringing to him. But, so help me, that old geezer wouldn't say mud if'n he had a mouthful. Can you explain to me why Mr. Diskin's so silent?"

Papa never answered a question fast. With luck, I might get a reply in the same week.

"Some folks," Papa later said, staring me straight with those farmer blue eyes of his that were fiercer than an eagle's, "say a ample lot more'n their prayers."

That was his answer.

It took decades, but I final decoded it.

And smiled. He'd meant *me*.

Then along came a certain Saturday. It was a dark, rainy November day that threatened a long winter. Soup and I, even though we didn't care to admit it, hadn't been too ambitious all week. Not at our farming chores, or in school, or in collecting enough tinfoil. We had two balls of it. Neither worth a dime.

"We need twenty cents," said Soup.

"Or," I said, "we don't have enough for two tickets. Maybe we just won't go."

We were on our way downroad, headed into town. The time was a minute or two beyond twelve noon.

"Rob," said Soup, "we can't miss seeing Stan Laurel and Oliver Hardy."

"No," I said, "I don't guess we can."

"Maybe," said Soup, "we could combine our two balls of foil into one. To look bigger. Like more."

We did.

But it didn't work too well. Our one ball of tinfoil looked pretty puny. Bending over, Soup picked up one of the many pebbles along the dirt roadway. In Vermont there's no shortage of rocks, large or small.

He tossed it into the air, and caught it.

"Rob," he said, "I just got a peachy idea."

"What is it?"

"All we do," he said, "is hide a tiny little pebble, this one here, inside our tinfoil. It'll look a mite bigger, weigh more, and now we won't have to worry about whether or not we'll get twenty cents for two movie tickets."

"It's cheating," I told Soup.

Soup stopped. "Don't you get it? Old man Diskin is a Jew. The other day I overheard a guy say that it's okay to cheat a Jew because the Jews cheat everybody else!"

"I never heard that before," I said.

"Well, that's all I heard. So maybe it'll be okay to cheat old Diskin."

I shook my head. "You know as well as I do that he's always been nice to us."

"We can't miss Laurel and Hardy. It's about a gorilla and a piano, somebody said."

Well, I didn't want to cheat Mr. Diskin, nor did I want to miss out seeing Stan Laurel and Oliver Hardy, who were my very favorite comedians.

"Okay," I said. "Just one time. Even if we get away with it, I don't guess I'll ever want to try it again."

We tried it. At the junkyard, Mr. Diskin tied a white hanky over his eyes as he sat behind a rusty set of scales. It was his only joke, pretending to be Justice, the blindfolded lady. My entire body was itching so bad that I could have sneezed down the shack. It was all I could do to keep myself from bolting out of there and running away.

Soup handed him our ball.

Mr. Diskin looked suddenly surprised. He wasn't wearing the hanky over his eyes when he disappeared into the back room, came back, and placed three tiny items on his counter.

Two dimes and a stone.

Our pebble.

I saw his mouth trembling, yet he still said nothing. His eyes were shiny wet, like tinfoil, and his face appeared very sad.

Soup and I looked at each other.

Then we ran.

I remember that awful Saturday like it happened only yesterday. We couldn't go to the movies. Nor did we want to. Instead, the two of us just walked and walked, saying nothing. Soup, I figured, was feeling as shameful as I felt, for being so dishonest to old Mr. Barney Diskin, who'd always been so kind.

I'm glad we didn't take his dimes.

# Early Pardee

MR. EARL PARDEE WAS A FRIEND OF MY FATHER, HAVEN Peck, and neighborly with my Uncle Charles and Uncle Edward.

No one called him Earl.

Instead, he got Early. I'd guess anybody in our part of Vermont could rightful recall how such a logical diminutive got spawned. We all remember, more or less, how Early was perpetuated.

Earl Pardee's trade was shoeing horses.

When called, he'd obligingly say, "All right, I'll come around to your place in the morning."

The horse owner would still be abed in the pitch of night and hear a sudden knock at the door. Opening it, he'd see Mr. Earl Pardee, smiling in the moonlight. "Do you know what time it is?" was the habitual question that so often greeted the caller.

43

Without waiting for Earl's answer, the unwilling host continued by muttering something like "It's only four o'clock."

"Yes," agreed Earl, "but that's morning to me, and it also be morning to your horse."

He was right. You don't have to be a genius to realize that a horse that's requiring hoofs cut and shoes reset is in a sooner-the-better mood. Even the city people know that much. However, you can't expect too many folks to wax intelligent at four bongs past midnight.

Early would crack a smile, parade in the front door as though invited, and ask, "What's for breakfast?"

At an hour before milking, Mr. Pardee did such at our place. Still rubbing his eyes, my father opened the door to darkness, and there stood good old Early, his face featuring both a grin and an appetite.

"Rob," said Mama, her hair down and her body up, "hustle out to the henhouse and fetch eggs." I started to leave. "Rag 'em off before you dare to enter the kitchen. Not after."

I hurried, aware of what my mother meant. Chickens never lay clean. A fresh egg, first off, is warm and wet. When it dries, it's speckled with dirt flecks that beg to be wiped tidy. I'd guess that people who think that eggs actual come from

grocery-store cartons presume different. So, following Mama's instructions, I went hastening to our
chicken coop, entered, and then had to apologize to
the local residents, who, unlike Early Pardee, didn't
quite agree that it was already morning.

"Easy," I said. "I'm sorry, ladies, so please excuse
me."

They didn't. Mistaking me for a stoat, our
Plymouth Rock matrons tuned up a chorus of
hysteria that was intended to discourage my stay. I
wasn't overfond of our chickens. For years they
had known who I was: the youngest Peck, assigned
to egg gathering and chicken manure disposal. A
hen with only half an eye could ascertain that I was
neither a ferret nor a fox.

"It's not my fault," I explained to an irate hen,
"because Mr. Pardee got here early. That's just his
way. And he expects a breakfast."

Romulus then disagreed. He was our Rhode
Island Red rooster, who, at the moment, hadn't
even considered hopping up to his favorite fence
post to emit a crow that usual cracked open a morning like you'd break an egg.

"Romulus," I said, "it's Mr. Pardee. Not me. He's
come to attend the mare, so it's no bother of yours,
you hear?"

In the past, Romulus and I had never established
what you might describe as a binding friendship.

Up until age five, I was afraid of him. At six, wary. At seven years, cautious enough to avoid any personal contact with those yellow spurs and beak, all three of which appeared to be able to puncture a little kid into an immediate state of total deflation.

Quickly, I grabbed the eggs, my hand darting beneath gray feathery abdomens in semi-repose at the laying boxes, feeling for fruit.

"Here's the eggs," I said to Mama, bursting into a lamplit kitchen where my mother was stoking a six-hundred-pound, coal-black Acme American cookstove into predawn performance.

Mr. Early Pardee, I noticed, was already occupying one of the eight chairs that surrounded our circular kitchen table. In his right hand, he held a fork. His left, an eager knife that was honed for hospitality.

"Ah," he said, eyeing the eggs.

Bacon, I smelled and heard, was already sizzling in a black iron spider—or, if you prefer, a skillet. With little ceremony, my mother split open egg after egg, whacked on the frypan's rim, then dropped into a destiny of bubbling bacon grease.

"I favor breakfast," said Early.

Mama responded, "So do I, but only in the morning."

Aunt Carrie was up too. Following her instruction, I began to peel a dozen potatoes, my paring knife flashing, reducing each brown giant into a white midget ready for frying.

"My," said Mama, noticing my undressed vegetation, "the potatoes were certain puny last summer." Each potato, however, was reduced even further to home-fry slices, which were cooked in the hot bacon grease.

She raised two dozen hot biscuits, which she served in a homemade wicker basket. Also a jar of home-dripped blackberry preserve and a dish of rhubarb conserve, topped off with a gallon of black and boiling coffee. Mama clamped a lid on breakfast with generous slabs of mincemeat pie. And home cheese.

Nobody left lighter or leaner from my mother's table.

Not even Early.

"A breakfast ain't a breakfast, Lucy," he told Mama, "without a piece of pie." He spread a wider grin. "Or maybe a extra helping."

To tell you the honest straight of it, there wasn't a Peck in all Vermont who'd deny a man like Mr. Early Pardee his justified eats. He was a good blacksmith. Horses trusted Earl. So did his customers. His work was prompt and perfect, so nobody had a cause to complain. Or a horse to limp.

After breakfast, and right following milking, Mr. Pardee allowed me to observe his ritual.

Winter or summer, Early Pardee would always shoe hot. One time he explained why. "A horse is like a woman, Robert. A horse wants to slide a hoof into a warm slipper, not to a curve of cold iron."

It was a pleasure to watch Early work. Never would he rush at a horse, but instead befriend the animal. From a pocket, he pulled out a long carrot. It looked more orange than usual because of the glow of his fire coals. Busting the carrot into three pieces, he fed our mare, himself, and me.

It tasted good.

Betsy, our mare, eyed him close, because Mr. Pardee wasn't one of the Peck family.

Bending over, he hefted up a hoof. "Robert, you always want to lift a front hoof first, even though it's maybe a rear shoe that got throwed. Here, up front, Betsy can watch me handle her some, feel how I do it, smell my smell, then decide if I'm to be trusted."

Walking to the tailgate of his wagon, Early hooked his arms under the anvil's points, then toted it to a stack of flat boards he'd previously prepared.

"A anvil," he told me, "ought to be the exact correct height. Not too high or too low down."

"How do you measure it?"

"Fetch me my hammer. I'll show you."

I brung it.

"Here's how." Standing at his anvil, he hung his right arm down to extend the hammer forward, on a level. "See? That's how a smith settles the proper height of his anvil table, so's it'll let his arm straighten full at the moment he strikes a blow. If the anvil's too high or too low, my arm'll tire out quick." He smiled at me. "Make sense?"

I nodded.

"Soft now, Betsy," he said. "A hour from now your hoofs are going to feel a lot more comforted."

As he worked, Early sang a little waltz. It was called "A Four-Footed Friend." I don't guess I can remember all of the words to it, but it ended "a four-footed, one-two-three-four-footed friend." Nobody could ever accuse Mr. Early Pardee of being a sweet singer. His voice sounded like maybe he gargled with gravel. Yet, when he sang "A Four-Footed Friend," it was somehow velvety as a mare's nose.

Working gentle, he scraped away some scurf grit off Betsy's hoof rim, wiping the hard, pulpy frog with a rag. Using pincers, he pried off the shoe, then pared the horn shorter. He tossed me a half-circle clipping of hoof and watched me catch it.

"Feel how wet and near-to-soft a hoof really is?" he asked me.

He was right.

"Believe it or not, Robert, I bet there's people

in this world who never bent up a horse's leg to examine what the underside of a hoof is really like. To me, hoofs favor folks. No two of 'em are twins. I never seen two hoofs alike."

Thinking about what Early Pardee had told me, I figured it held a smack of truth.

"Never," he said, "purchase a hard-hoofed horse. If you do, chances are his nature'll be equal steely. A brain like barbed wire."

He made one more smooth cut around the entire rim of Betsy's hoof.

Edging in closer to cop a look, I asked, "How much do you know to shave off?"

Without glancing up, he answered. "Just enough to allow her frog to hop, to take the shock off her legs. The frog'll bounce her gait so she don't drag-trot. Horses are same as people. When your feet hurt, ya ache all over."

Early burned a shoe red in his fire; then, holding it with tongs, he clanged it on the anvil with his hammer.

Before his asking me to do it, I fetched him a bucket full of water. Well, not really full up, but mostly. As he dunked in the red iron, a hiss popped up to match the steam.

"There," he said. "That's a warm slipper, Betsy."

Fitting the hot shoe to her filed foot, he pounded in all the nails. When her foot was flat rested on the ground, I could see the sharp nail points poking up through the top of her hoof, until Earl twisted off each one with a pair of shorter tongs. Now all I saw was a neat silvery row.

"They look like little stars," I said.

To my surprise, Early stared at me, saying nary a thing, just looking. At last, he finally spoke. "That's what my wife said to me once. Just as you done. Like the twisted-off nails were stars."

"I'm sorry Mrs. Pardee died," I said. Because he'd lost his wife a year before.

Early wiped his wet face. "Yeah, me too. Some days I ponder what's keeping me alive. Why I go on living alone, and lonesome." He patted Betsy. "Funny thing, I don't usual talk about Martha May to nobody." He sighed. "At home, I still keep her slippers under our bed. They're so little and pink. Yet I keep 'em there with me, hoping she'll come back again."

Early didn't say much more.

He merely continued to work while I watched. Then, after Papa paid him his due, he doused the fire, loaded his anvil and tools to his wagon bin, and left our Betsy with a warm iron slipper on every hoof.

As I went to sleep that night, I could picture a pair of small pink slippers beneath the bed of a very strong and gentle man.

# Miss Kelly

SHE EARNED THIRTEEN DOLLARS A WEEK.

Where? In a red-brick one-room schoolhouse on a Vermont clay road. She was the only teacher I knew for six years.

Behind her orderly desk, on an unpainted wall, an angular needlepoint plaque hung from a crooked nail:

SCHOLARSHIP,
MANNERS, AND SOAP

We were marched to the washstand if we smelled dirty, appeared dirty, or talked dirty. Whenever we were in the wrong, Miss Kelly knew it and we knew it. Discipline did not require discussion.

Octagon soap solved many a problem. Even now, whenever I cuss, I can still taste it on my tongue.

Miss Kelly read us *Ivanhoe* and *Tom Sawyer* and *The Wind in the Willows*.

On my very first trip to Rutland, the only nearby town of any size, an aunt (knowing my liking for books) pointed at a downtown structure. "Look there, Robert. That's a library."

Shaking my head in disbelief, I knew it wasn't. Because we had a library in our schoolroom. It was a short wooden plank nailed in one corner of the room, upon which sat our two dozen books. Well chosen and well worn. To me, a library couldn't be a building. It was a piece of wood.

A library board.

Miss Kelly had a rule: Only clean hands were allowed to touch our precious prizes.

If we objected or sulked at Octagonal discipline, Miss Kelly used her term of explanation. Standing very erect, she'd utter her favorite word:

"Standards."

At the time, we students were the poorly dressed sons and daughters of farmers, widows, hog butchers, paper millers, and lumberjacks. Most of our parents were illiterate, early aged by brutal work and bitter winters. Our teacher collected old newspapers from her neighbors, brought them to school, sometimes read parts of them to us, and stuffed them flat inside our shirts and home-knit sweaters on sub-zero days.

Weather, in Vermont, was always a popular subject because we had so dreadful much of it. Miss Kelly explained to the twenty-eight of us that every year has four seasons: spring, summer, fall, and winter. Raising my hand, I told our teacher, "Mama says there's only *two* seasons in Vermont. She claims there's just *winter* and *canning.*"

It made Miss Kelly smile. "Robert," she said, regaining her usual dignity, "your mother is also correct."

We learned to read and to write. But we were never to feel ashamed, Miss Kelly often warned us, that our mothers or fathers could do neither. "Jesus," she said, "was a carpenter's son, and He probable never went to school."

I recall one dreadful day.

Miss Kelly had been reading us poems. A poem, she informed us, was merely a song without music. And a person didn't have to be British to be a soldier like Oliver Cromwell, a sea captain such as Lord Nelson, or a poet. Anyone could write one. Even children. "Tonight," she commanded us, "I'm asking each of you to compose a poem."

We groaned beneath the burden of this impossible task.

"Following chores and supper," Miss Kelly said, "sit quietly at your kitchen table and write about something you know. Show it to me. And allow my hands, as I read your poem tomorrow, to touch the warmth of your cow. Or pet your dog. Take me to your own barn. Let me see your calf. Hear your chickens. Or taste your cow's warm fresh morning milk."

None of us said *boo*.

Miss Kelly smiled. "Do your best," she said, "and an angel can do no better."

Before leaving the school that afternoon, each of us received two sheets of paper and a stubby pencil from our teacher. Many a local residence lacked such luxuries. Upon arriving home, I found Mama in our kitchen (our main room for cooking, washing clothes or kids, eating, and entertaining). My mother stood where she so often did. At our sink. I told her my problem, showing her the pencil and paper, and expressing that I had no idea whatsoever for my poem.

"Sarah's probable out to the barn," Mama said, "with her new batch of kittens. They're all so precious pretty, you could write a *song* about them. Her kittens are so wondrous and Miss Sarah's so proud."

My mother was again right.

That evening, I did my very first piece of

writing. Having recently learned the word *won-drous,* I figured it applied, and composed my poem.

I titled it "Sarah's Wondrous Thing."

Next morning, I handed it in to Miss Kelly. She looked at it, along with all twenty-seven others. Pulling open her desk drawer, she extracted a little box, and then licked a tiny gold star to press on my paper. It was my first gold star. But then came the bad part. I had to stand up front, face my classmates, and read my poem . . . in my itchy underwear and with Norma Jean Bissell watching.

### SARAH'S WONDROUS THING

Sarah is our tabby cat,
And always every spring,
She steals away out to the barn
And does a wondrous thing.

Somehow, she has some kittens
In the hay up in the loft.
They all don't look like Sarah
But they touch so wondrous soft.

Each day I hurry home from school
And up the barnyard path.
And there is Sarah giving each
And every one a bath.

Sarah licks each tiny ear
And tiny tail of silk.
Then they have their supper,
Which is really Sarah's milk.

I don't know how she does it,
But she does it every spring.
It makes me want to whistle,
'Cause it's such a wondrous thing.

At the end of the school day we all lined up, like usual, to shake hands with Miss Kelly before being paroled into freedom's compelling call.

I was last in line.

"Good night, Miss Kelly," I said, as I had said hundreds of earlier times.

"Good night, Robert." Her hand brushed my face. Leaning over an inch or two toward me, she said softly, "I think you might do more in this world than kill hogs."

She knew about Papa's part-time job. After saying it, she almost seemed to be sorry that it had slipped out. Then she told me that teachers and farmers did a similar sort of work. Both were raisers, in charge of the green and growing.

"A farmer," she told me, "gets up and goes to his garden." She smiled. "But I'm luckier. My garden comes to me."

So much of what I learned for six years in that one room has stayed with me. In mind, and in heart. She was my free pass from poverty. Because of Miss Kelly, I've included her three values of Scholarship, Manners, and Soap in more than one novel. A lot more.

And shared them with Anne and Christopher.

My children.

# A Tender Man

HIS FACE WAS BLACKENED BY COAL.

Working a job like his, using a shovel to stoke coal from the tender into the boiler fire of a loco-motive, no one could remain clean. There was always a rag or bandanna tied around his neck.

The train didn't come every day.

Ours was a rural area of Vermont, during the Great Depression of the 1930s. Even in boom times (nobody could recall too many of those), the freight train was rarely longer than a score of cars.

I remember bringing an empty burlap bag to school. After final recess, I'd separate myself from the other children in order to visit the water tower at the grade crossing. Here was a place where the giant black engine would slow and then shudder to a dead stop. And hiss. Clouds of vapor billowed from beneath the long horizontal boiler.

In winter (because of the season, mountains, and latitude), it was promising dark by four o'clock. As there was very little light at the water tower, I had to feel around for lumps of coal to bring home. If I heard the train whistle, I'd wait. It took a long time for the creeping freight to arrive. But worthy of the waiting. Its jerky stop loosened lumps of coal from the tender, just behind the engine. With fortune, I could fill my burlap sack with more fuel than I could drag to where we lived.

Every inch was an uproad trek.

Sometimes there was no coal at all on the ground. The engineer, who throttled the train, never seemed to notice. If so, he didn't care. But his partner, the fireman, would always contribute on the sly. Once in a while I'd prompt him, holding up my empty bag, hoping he'd see me.

The fireman and I had a secret code between us that I figured his boss (the engineer) didn't know. Somehow the tender guy managed to spill a few black lumps. They tumbled downward to freckle the fresh snow.

It made no sense to try to yell up a "Thank you, Mister," because of the locomotive's persistent noise.

But I waved, and he waved back. Or sort of threatened me with the handle of his shining shovel.

During my boyhood, the railroad must have donated half a ton of coal to our big black six-hundred-pound Acme American kitchen stove. Free coal baked a bunch of biscuits for the Peck family.

I was hoping that the fireman (the tender man) wouldn't be found out and given the boot due to his benevolence. Because it was, after all, the railroad company's coal, not the fireman's to give away. The fireman, however, had a way of protecting his job. After spilling a few lumps of coal, his custom was to yell down at me. Fisting a hand to tell me to keep away from the tracks and to vacate the railroad's right-of-way property. Don't ask me how I figured he didn't mean all of his hostile words or gestures. I just knew. Even though I never learned his name.

At night, especially after hauling home a half-full bag, I'd always remember the locomotive fireman in my prayers. I never forgot the tender man because he never forgot me.

Years later, I drove my car to the grade crossing, stopped, got out, and inhaled a black memory. Now, beneath my feet, there were no lumps of coal for a kid to lug home. None at all. The coal tender was gone because the locomotive engine was no longer steam. It was now a diesel. An oil burner.

Perhaps there are trains up in Heaven.

Maybe, instead of diesel engines or electricity,

the Holy Heaven R.R. still rolls behind smoking coal-burners, with an engineer and a very tender man for a fireman. One who wastes a few nuggets of coal for cold children who have an empty burlap bag.

I pray his face is finally clean.

# Keepsake

Soup Vinson heard the news.

He told me. At the time, Luther Wesley Vinson was eleven. And I was ten.

It's an age when frisky boys consider climbing the rickety stairs that lead to what we imagined as maturity. Manhood, our adolescence reasoned, was possessing not qualities or virtues, but tangible trinkets of proof to show off to our less-advanced contemporaries. For example, matches and stubby Lucky Strike butts. Or a handy pocket opener to flick caps off bottles of beer not yet acquired, or even an acquired taste.

Soup and I were veteran drinkers of sweet apple cider. From a jug!

However, the latest fad, a few high school giants informed us, was carrying a particular grown-up article in one's pocket, solid evidence that you were *one of the guys.*

This coveted equipment, so recently in fashion, could be quietly purchased at the drugstore, but only by adults. Or big boys. Kids like us, even with money in hand, would be rejected and dejected customers. Not only that. Twerps who tried would probably be laughed at. Or worse, reported to their parents.

There was, according to rumor, a new secret coin machine. Only one of its kind in town. This mechanical marvel was located on the wall of the men's room down the road at the Diesel Fuel. Here the prize was available to all. Its price was a quarter. No pennies, nickels, or dimes (items that dominated our savings) were accepted. Quarters only. The dispenser didn't sell penny gumballs.

This machine was big-time!

Soup and I casually sneaked into the Diesel Fuel's only restroom, bolted the door, looked around, and there it was. A foreign rectangular object hung on the wall, up high, flashing the brand name of its forbidden fruit:

TROJAN

Earlier, we'd cashed in our long-collected small change, a total of twenty-five cents, and now were financially prepared. Inside my clenched fist I felt our quarter, burning hot, panting for adventure.

Reverently, we read the instructions:

1. Quarters only.
2. Insert quarter in slot.
3. Select type desired.
4. Pull lever completely down.
5. Package will appear in tray.

Clearly printed, easy-to-follow directions. But a problem had suddenly confronted us. Select type desired? The selection was made, we then learned upon closer examination of the machine's technical demands, by pushing one of its three flaming-red buttons:

a. American Hero
b. French Tickler
c. Arabian Stallion

The American Hero style, we concluded, lacked a certain man-of-the-world appeal. Yet choosing between the two remaining choices was no snap-judgment decision. It required that Soup and I exchange our vast reservoirs of romantic sophistication and social experience, weighing all opinions of French or Arab behavior.

"Maybe," said Soup, "we ought to flip a coin."

"Okay," I agreed. "Heads it's French, and tails it's Arabian."

"You flip," Soup told me, "and I'll catch it."

An errant toss, plus a fumbled catch, and our precious quarter went jingling to the concrete floor, then rolled across the dampness to underneath the toilet tank. Down on our knees, in unpleasant moistures and aromas, we groped for our twenty-five cents. "I can see it," Soup said, "but I can't quite seem to reach it."

*Whack. Whack.*

Somebody was outside the door!

"Hey, anybody in there?" asked a trucky male voice. "Open up. Or else."

"What'll we do?" I whispered too loudly.

"Be right out," Soup croaked in a wavering soprano.

The trucker said a colorful word. A real zinger. "You kids got no right to be in there. Hurry up and come on out. And pronto."

With a desperate ram of my hand into an area about which I knew (or wanted to know) nothing, I managed to reclaim the quarter, dirt and all. Rising, I inserted the gritty coin in the machine's slot as Soup hurriedly mashed a button. At this point, any selection would do. I yanked down the lever. After a click, and an eternity of a full second, down into the tray thumped our prize, an American Hero Trojan.

Patriotism had triumphed over exotica.

*WHACK!*

"Open that door," threatened an irate voice, "or I'll bust it down and throttle you kids. And I mean now!"

We opened the door. There stood a beefy trucker, holding a quarter. Behind him, seated in the cab of his truck, a lady was shouting a suggestion.

"Hurry it up, Harry. I only got half an hour."

"In a minute, Gladice. Okay?"

Soup and I decided not to wait around to offer Harry any advice on what, of the three selections, he should purchase. We ran like flushed rabbits. I felt my face blushing with guilt, fearing that Soup and I would be caught and jailed for life. A bold headline on the front page of our local Weekly would trumpet the tawdry news to the entire world:

TROJAN BUYERS NABBED!

After a brief shoot-out, the Vermont Vice Squad announced that two underage criminals, Luther Wesley Vinson and Robert Newton Peck, were apprehended on Saturday as the pair were trying to make their escape from a daring daylight shopping spree in the men's restroom of the Diesel Fuel Truck Stop. Evidence was confiscated, marked, and identified as a package of American Hero. Both convicts are shackled, hand and foot, to await trial in a solitary maximum-security dungeon. The District Attorney expects a sure life-sentence conviction, claiming he has a key witness, a trucker named Harry, and another possible observer, who pleaded not to be identified and not to mention anybody named Gladice.

We ran for at least a mile.

Over fences, through bull pastures, splashing through a shallow crick and then pulling up to breathe.

A close call.

We stashed our American Hero in a variety of remote locations: Stoddard's Ice House, under a rain barrel behind Higbee's Hardware, and in assorted nooks known only to us.

Unfamiliar with Vermont's codified Statute of

Limitations, we waited and played it cool, spurning the folly of flashing the take of our caper to any of our socially underachieving classmates. After several nervous weeks, we concluded that the proverbial coast was clear. At last we could offer our American Hero its long-awaited debut.

Its virgin excursion came on a Saturday night in May. As customary, we were allowed to come to town with our parents, wearing our good shirts, and promenade to and fro along a very short Main Street, to strut with the concealed confidence that Trojan ownership provides, and to give all the chicks a chance to admire our swaggering masculinity.

We took turns carrying the American Hero.

Having noticed where the high school boys packed theirs, we did likewise. Inside the right front pocket of blue jeans there's another tiny pocket, about two inches square. Our mothers told us that this was a watch pocket. We both, however, knew its true purpose. It was where a tiger tucks a Trojan.

Days passed, and then weeks, the inevitable changing of seasons, year after year. Several pairs of blue jeans were outworn and outgrown, yet my American Hero managed to adjust to the transition for close to a decade. There it rode, secure in its denim cockpit, ready to serve its ultimate purpose if ever the opportunity presented. Originally (we opened the package and peeked) it was white. But as the years flew by, it yellowed, turned green, and darkened into decay.

There wasn't another American Hero Trojan ever vulcanized that provided more pleasure than this one. Neither a French Tickler nor an Arabian Stallion. Mine, by sheer rubbery endurance, stretched time into a championship of chastity.

At age seventeen, prior to entering the Army, I considered taking it with me. For an enlisted soldier, it seemed that one American hero might luck out and employ another.

Instead, I stowed it among my assorted souvenirs of youth, left it behind, and marched away to war.

Upon returning, I found it. The aging process had taken its toll. My perennial American Hero had retired to little more than a puny parcel of dust. Perhaps, I mused, I'd offer it to the Smithsonian, finally to prove my manhood.

Yet it isn't easy to part with a cherished keepsake.

Though I considered establishing an Old Trojan's Home, I didn't relish the thought of having either Mama or Aunt Carrie learn the sordid truth of my reckless and feckless past. So, with an appropriate ceremony, I dug a hole and buried it.

There, beneath the pristine Vermont topsoil, an American Hero still lies, a silent tribute to my un-intended innocence, a monument to an eventual moral revolution that I had inadvertently spawned.

I had conceived Safe Sex.

# Joe

No one really knew him.

Or wanted to, because he smelled worse than a wet barn dog. Yet everyone in town recognized him.

Joe was an orphan. If he'd had parents, they'd up and disappeared years ago. Few people knew or cared how old Joe Galipo was. Perhaps not even Joe himself. Bone scrawny, he was close to my size; I was coming up ten or eleven.

Miss Noe, the constable's sister, would sometimes feed Joe, scrub him, burn or bury his filthy clothes, and supply him with a fresh outfit from the back-room stockpile at the Methodist church. Her brother, whenever he could collar him, escorted Joe to our school. Miss Kelly allowed Joe to sit anywhere he wanted: in winter, near the black upright woodstove, and in spring, close to the door. Whenever her back was turned, he ran away.

Joe lived anywhere and everywhere, surviving any way he could. People claim he stole food, yet few could righteously object.

He tried to keep out of sight.

Rarely would he appear on Main Street. His home, if it could be called that, was a back alley. Joe moved in shadows, darting from one hiding place to another. Rather than being a child, he was a stray cat.

Miss Noe claimed that Joe would talk to her. But on any rare day when he was in school, he never spoke word one.

Joe was considered simple. People used the word *slow*. Because he was thought to be the village fool, nobody offered to adopt him, or take him inside. Time and again, Joe Galipo was chased out of barns for fear he'd stupidly light a match in the straw. In cold weather, Joe added layers and layers of clothing items around his body. When frightened, he ran, his rags flapping like broken wings.

A few of our local youngsters were cruel to Joe, cornering him to bully. To them, it was a kind of outdoor sport. Seeing this made me angry, but I was too small to do much about it. Except yell.

Joe Galipo never talked to me until I started giving him eats. I wouldn't walk up to Joe and hand him anything. But once I discovered one of the places where he slept, behind the boarded-up old Opera House, I'd leave an apple, a raw potato, or a tin can full of fresh milk nearby, where I figured he'd find it.

Once I found the empty milk can with a penny in it. A silent payment.

"Thank you, Joe," I hollered behind the Opera House. "I'm Rob."

I sort of guessed, or hoped, he heard me. Soon after, he let me see him and didn't run away. He just stood in his soiled garb and stared. I smiled at him, raised my hand to a howdy, and Joe smiled back. When I tossed him a cucumber, he dropped it, stooped to retrieve it, and scurried off.

Perhaps, I reasoned, Joe wasn't stupid. Just silent. Maybe because he might be deaf. I was wrong. Joe Galipo could hear, and speak. He just didn't have any cause. When I asked Miss Noe about him, she told me that Joe could talk, and was possible smarter than a lot of our other citizens. But then she explained that Joe didn't converse with a normal voice. He had a stammer. Miss Noe thought it was because Joe was afraid.

Joe wasn't the only Galipo in town.

We had two families of them, living over by the lead mill, close to the crick. The Galipo kids, both families, weren't very friendly. And to Joe they were meaner than a sin on Sunday. His worst enemies.

Miss Noe claimed they considered Joe an embarrassment, giving any other Galipo a bad name. To them, Joe was just a dirty joke.

Years passed.

When I was thirteen, Papa died, and we lost our farm soon after. Then there was only Mama and Aunt Carrie, and me. A good neighbor stopped by with an empty wagon. We loaded what little we had and moved into town, into two tiny rooms above a feed store. Mama found work, taking care of two elderly women. I took odd jobs. Aunt Carrie took sick.

We squeaked by.

As often as possible, I still sneaked food to Joe Galipo. We got to be friends. I handled most of our conversations. Joe didn't have anything to say, but I knew he trusted me. One afternoon, Joe got roughed up by some of our local thugs. I found him in the alley, alone, curled up on the gritty ground and holding his belly like it hurt.

"I'm your friend, Joe," I told him.

He actual spoke my name.

"Rob . . . you an' Miss Noe. You're . . . you're my only friends." His voice sounded puny. The words didn't come out very plain, but at least he was saying something. "I got a secret," he told me. "Do you want to see it? But don't tell nobody about my secret thing. I never tell Miss Noe."

"Where is it?"

"Come on," he said. "I'll show ya."

I followed him.

Behind the beat-up old Opera House, a place that hadn't been open to the public since I could ever recall, Joe loosened a few rotted boards. We crawled inside. It was dark, spooky, and smelled musty. My face met a spiderweb. Secret or no secret, all I wanted was to leave.

"I sleep here," Joe said. "And it's where I talk. Alone. I talk all the time. Like people."

Moving more boards, Joe allowed some light to sift inside. As my eyes adjusted, I saw we were on some sort of a stage. There were ratty curtains and hanging ropes.

"Here," said Joe. "Here it is." I watched him remove a large tarp of canvas off what appeared to be a big box. He lifted up a lid. "It's my piano," Joe said.

There it was. Joe Galipo had a piano but no family. I had a family and no piano. It made me smile. Nobody gets it all.

"I can play it, Rob."

Blinking at him in disbelief, I asked, "You can?"

He could. Joe sat on a bench, placed his hands on the black-and-white keys, and played a little song. Something I'd never heard. It sounded pretty as flowers. All the way through to the end.

"Wow," I said. "That's really good. How'd you learn to play a piano? Who taught you?"

"Me."

"You taught yourself to play it?"

Joe nodded. "It's so easy. The hard part was fixing all the sour noise." He showed me an old pair of pliers. "With these. Took a long time to tight up the wires inside. But I done it, so all the sounds mix together." He grinned at me. "You wanna learn?"

"Boy, *do* I."

"Watch. And listen. It helps to look at first. But now I don't have to look no more. I can play at night."

"Show me again."

Joe's left hand played a low note.

"Down yonder," he said, "is the father. See where my little finger is? Then, five notes up, is the mother. Press 'em down together and they get married." It sounded like a bagpipe. Yet it was correct, as if Joe actually knew how to do it. And how to teach me. With his right hand, Joe played a few higher notes. Three, then four. "Up here. These are the children. All together, they'll make up a family. They're my family now. Hear 'em? They all love each other."

The way he explained it, in such a sweet way, made me almost want to cry.

As we stood on that dirty old stage, the piano

wasn't so important anymore. Joe sat there, moving his hands around, playing one family after another. The father and mother sounded so strong, and the higher-up kids so happy. They tinkled away like laughter.

Day after day, Joe taught me how to play his piano. We made up our own melodies. He had given names to many of the notes on the keyboard. Below, fathers and mothers, plus uncles and aunts and grandparents. Above, his brothers and sisters, nieces, nephews. Some of Joe's notes were puppies and kittens. And away up top sounded the mice and sparrows.

I learned to play. By ear, the Joe Method. Today I can play anything I hear. Duke Ellington, Gershwin, Cole Porter, and my favorite, Scott Joplin's century-old ragtime and blues.

What happened to Joe?

I don't know. Returning home from the U.S. Army (an enlisted high-school dropout) after World War II, I scouted around for my former friends and located most of them. But no Joe. The old unused Opera House, originally built right after the Civil War, had been torn down and carted away to make space for a Piggly Wiggly. And now even that is no longer there.

Miss Noe was elderly, bless her heart, and

couldn't remember either one of us. Or even her brother.

Well, wherever you are, Mr. Joe Galipo, I hope you have music, and a home where there are songs of laughter and kindness. Plus a whole bunch of kin. Lots of notes with names. On that day long ago when I learned about Joe's talent and brains, I also discovered his true secret, what he longed for most of all.

It wasn't a piano.

# Part II
# Early Manhood

# Mr. Gene Autry

IT WAS 1945.

I was a proud seventeen-year-old private in the United States Army. I'd enlisted but didn't yet need a razor. About to be shipped overseas.

There was another soldier in our unit, a corporal, who had a cousin who knew Gene Autry. I mean really *knew* him. Mr. Autry, even though many times a millionaire, had also enlisted and soldiered a few years in Burma. He now had an Honorable Discharge and was about to resume his astounding career in Hollywood.

Corporal Smith told us that his cousin could persuade Gene to visit our camp.

Nobody believed him.

Until that unforgettable evening when we assembled, and guess who appeared. A gentleman who (before he retired) was a cowboy star in almost

Age seventeen, en route to WWII Italy.

one hundred movies. As a child, I recalled seeing Gene Autry's records featured in full-page listings in every Sears Roebuck mail-order catalog. And now here he was, in person. With us.

Mr. Gene Autry.

He wore rather plain cowboy duds, nothing with fringe or spangles. Waving his guitar to a thousand cheering guys, he stood on some crates and boxes, a makeshift stage, and charmed us. Mostly with songs about home.

He sang "Mexicali Rose." It's a waltz about returning to a pretty gal, a back-home somebody to love and miss, and maybe never to see again.

"You're the Only Star in My Blue Heaven" was next. More of the same. One heart longing to be true to another, far away.

Gene told us that his raising was in a little old place called Tioga, in Texas. He liked baseball and attempted to play a saxophone, but switched to a guitar because he so enjoyed singing. His grandpa had been a Baptist minister. I'd lost my own pa when I was thirteen. You might understand how much I appreciated Gene's song "That Silver-Haired Daddy of Mine."

In honor of his grandfather, Gene asked us if we'd mind hearing one or two of his favorite hymns. Nobody objected. He sang "Amazing Grace" and "What a Friend We Have in Jesus."

Plenty of big strong guys were sobbing.

There was a shine in Gene's eyes too. No one yelled, or hooted out any smart-mouth remarks. A war has a way of bringing men closer to God, and closer to one another. I recall placing a hand on the shoulder of a buddy who sat beside me and was wiping his eyes.

Gene told us about Champion, his black horse. He called him Champ a lot. We listened as though it were a prayer meeting.

In the front row, a young, small-of-stature soldier relaxed, closed his eyes, and drifted off to dreamland. Gene noticed him and grinned, placing a finger on his lips, asking us not to disturb him. Then he sang the slumbering little soldier a special lullaby: "Go to Sleep, My Little Buckaroo."

He told us that he couldn't sing it near as well as another cowboy, Mr. Dick Foran.

Listening, we were no longer stationed at an army post. Instead, we were little boys again, going to sleep in a familiar bed, hearing our mothers hum. Gene Autry let us fondly remember the purity of childhood, though none of us could ever return. To you, it may sound corny. But I was there, my dears, and that evening was as genuine as the corn on my father's farm.

Sweet corn.

If you're inclined, you ought to refresh your spirit sometime and listen to the music of Mr. Gene Autry.

He was a lot more man than a war hero and a rodeo rider. For us, it was almost as good as a furlough. And it tasted better than any beer in a barroom.

Gene also had an easy way of making us all laugh, especially when telling us about how he was first learning to pluck a guitar. A pal came ambling along, winced, and said to him, "Gene, unless you quit pickin' that thing, it'll never heal."

He told us about his comic sidekick and friend, Mr. Smiley Burnette, a chubby guy who was known on the screen as a character named Frog Millhouse. One time, just for laughs, Smiley rode a white sway-back horse in a rodeo parade. Later he met up a pretty gal.

"Did you see me in the parade?" Smiley asked her.

"Yup," she said, "I saw ya."

"Well, did I make a big impression?"

"Yeah," she replied. "On the *horse.*"

Gene said it was all so amusing that they decided to include that bit in a movie, and did.

Years earlier, Gene told us, another famous cowboy was one of the people who encouraged him. The cowboy's name? Mr. Will Rogers. Will, according to Gene, could really spin a rope and make it whistle.

Gene sang "Tumbling Tumbleweeds" and "Carolina Moon."

He said that Smiley Burnette could sing too, and doggone well. Smiley could do a real funny song entitled "Oh, I'm Going Back to the Backwoods."

Gene wouldn't sing it, though, because he claimed it was Frog's highlight and he couldn't do it justice. There was nothing uppity about Gene Autry. He admitted that he could ride and rope but couldn't act worth a spit.

But we knew one truth about that gentleman. He was a star!

At the end of his presentation, Gene sang the song that most everybody remembers his doing: "Back in the Saddle Again." If any cowboy tune could be a prayer for a bunch of homesick servicemen, and women as well, this was it. He sang it really slow. His benediction.

> "I'm back in the saddle again.
> Out where a friend is a friend . . ."

I was seventeen.

Now I am over seventy, but I can still hear the lyrics to the magnificent ballad, sung by the grandson of a Baptist preacher, and be baptized back into boyhood. A pity, but I never got to crowd forward and shake Gene's hand on that special evening, to offer him my personal gratitude. Best I do it here and now, even though the star is in his Blue Heaven.

Thank you, Mr. Gene Autry, for being able to make a lot of men feel like back-home boys.

# Dear Elliot

I MET HIM AT THE TAIL END OF WORLD WAR II.

Elliot was eighteen. And I was seventeen.

He hailed from a hometown with a funny name. The Bronx. At first, I figured it had something to do with rodeo stock (broncs), until Elliot explained that it was mostly a zoo. His pa, Elliot told me, was a presser in the garment district. Mine had killed hogs.

Were you to take a charcoal and paper and sketch a 4-F (an Army reject), you'd have Private Elliot Leftowitz, a born civilian. Short, squat, behind fogged glasses with lenses thicker than the bottom of Coke bottles. His pupils were twin hockey pucks. Somehow, he'd been drafted and inducted. A military miracle.

Between the pair of us, he was the one who shaved, but only following a very convincing request from Sergeant Malliniak.

Elliot, I suspected, doubted my sanity and was forever asking me the same question: "You enlisted?"

We endured Basic Training at picturesque Fort McClellan in Alabama, both of us in olive drab, in keeping with the current fashion that season. Elliot was issued an M1 rifle. They never got along. Everyone else stood at attention with heels together, toes apart. Elliot placed his toes together, heels spread. An only child, he'd never before been away from home. When marching, always at the rear of our platoon, he looked around curiously, blinking, squinting, bumping into things and apologizing.

Sergeant Malliniak called him "the tourist."

Elliot often received a letter from his mother. He shared all of her letters with me upon learning that my mother was illiterate and wouldn't be writing.

> Dear Elliot . . .
> Don't touch any guns. Unless you plan to grow up and become a criminal. Be sure to eat. If you're hungry at night, remind the sergeant that I'm a taxpayer and he should fix you a snack.

Sergeant Emil Malliniak never fixed us snacks. He fixed bayonets. He was from a bayou in

Mississippi, and when he barked out a nasal order, neither Elliot nor I had a clue as to what he wanted us to perform. So we both jumped around like crazy, pretending we understood.

"Rob," Elliot whispered to me in the barracks late one night, "I found us an interpreter."

"Can we eat it?"

"No," said Elliot. "I got us a guy from Mississippi, in the next bunk already." (Elliot ended sentences with *already,* but don't ask me why. He was rarely *all ready* for anything.) "He understands when Sergeant Malliniak snorts."

Sergeant Malliniak had a lot to say. I did whatever he ordered willingly, as he had become (his term) our Mother Hen. It took a while, but eventually I realized that our sergeant was married to the U.S. Army, and we were his only children.

Side by side, Elliot and I crawled on our bellies beneath sagging loops of barbed wire, over field dirt, as live rounds of cadre-fired ammunition hissed and whined twenty inches above our steel-helmeted heads. It was here that Elliot met, head-on and face to face, his first Alabama scorpion. Elliot was the scorpion's first Bronxite.

Both parties appeared unprepared for a social.

Elliot, who was a decent guy with all the practical intelligence of a crouton, decided that he'd best stand up and run. All I could think to do I did, smashing the butt of my rifle into Elliot's brainless helmet, knocking senseless the only buddy I had in the entire United States Army.

Somehow we survived.

"You enlisted?" he kept asking me.

Day after exhausting day, I managed to drag our unlikely warrior through swamps, up ropes, and over walls. On the rifle range I could be of little help. Elliot's right cheek was bruised and discolored from the mule-kick recoil of his M1 Garand weapon. His feet were swollen from marching, soft pinky hands blistered by heat and close-order drill, his body purpled by bayonet practice. Butt strokes.

He took it on the chin.

> Dear Elliot . . .
>
> Be sure to get to bed early, and sleep late. Are you taking the vitamins I sent you? Do not get your feet wet. Who is this Rob person you mentioned in your letter, the one who hunted back home and knows guns? He sounds like a gangster.

Following our evening with Gene Autry, we shipped overseas. To where, we didn't know.

"Maybe," said Elliot, "we'll get to shoot Japs."

He paused. "I'd hate to shoot anybody like Mrs. Katayama. She's on our block. Her name means Half Mountain."

It wasn't the *Queen Mary*. It was the U.S.A.T. (United States Army Transport) *Wilson Victory*, accommodating one thousand corn-fed and homesick lads who hadn't ventured across a body of water larger than a duck pond . . . or Central Park Lake.

Belowdecks, in the bowels of the ship, our cots were tightly formed in units of two dozen each, four together stacked six bunks high. I drew a bottom bunk, underneath five of the most seasick G.I.'s in the Army. As our vessel rolled and tossed through the North Atlantic, we vomited into our steel helmets. But only when our aim was accurate.

We docked at a somewhere called Livorno, in Italy, replacements for General Mark Clark's Fifth Army, the 88th Infantry Division, the Blue Devils.

Elliot and I started scouting for Japs.

Because of my proven experience with weaponry, I was soon assigned to be a machine gunner—a .30-caliber light (air-cooled) automatic M1919A1 with a mount M2—and Elliot was one of my ammo bearers. Instead of Germans or Italians, we battled the Yugoslavians (Jugs, we called them), who, under Marshal Tito and backed up by Russia, wanted to invade and claim a hunk of a weakened and demoralized Italy.

Our battlefront was the Morgan Line.

The weather wasn't sunny Italy. It was rainy, and cold. Food was sorry. A few among us received packages from home.

I was lucky to be Elliot's buddy.

With one reservation. Salami. Back in the Bronx, in Mama Leftowitz's spotless and busy kitchen, I'm sure her salami was fragrant enough. Already. However, due to distance and postal delays, by the time it caught up to the 88th Infantry her salami had ripened into a deadly weapon. It was unfit for human consumption, so naturally we offered it to Sergeant Malliniak, who, I by now concluded, could chew and digest artillery shell casings.

Even he refused.

Elliot and I devoured his mother's macaroons (Passover cookies), which, I observed, arrived by the carload. Her salami remained virginal and untouched. Not even Elliot, whose prime instruction during childhood was to *eat*, partook. Instead, he briefly unwrapped the salami, inhaled its revered back-home aroma, and said, "Guys, that's a breeze over the Bronx."

Our feet suffered.

Due to being continually cold and wet (and

a constant shortage of dry socks), our feet tended to turn blue, then black and crusty hard. With little or no feeling. It's called trench foot. I held Elliot in my arms as a medic, with forceps, took off one of his toes. I was luckier. But my right foot is still scarred.

> Dear Elliot . . .
>
> Pray God you receive this box of medicine. All kinds. You know your asthma condition, so try not to inhale any foreign air. At least here in New York we can see what's to breathe. If in doubt, take two of every pill I've enclosed.

At the time, I didn't know what *hypochondriac* meant. Elliot, I'm now sure, invented the word. Along with thirty pounds of machine gun ammunition, Elliot also toted his personal pharmacy of assorted medication. As to diseases or disorders or distresses, you name it, Elliot claimed *he had it* and was pill-prepared. Our platoon's physician-in-residence could, and did, dispense everything from dandruff shampoo to foot powder.

He even carried Midol.

In Italy, the mountains are steep, especially

when foggy and wet. Machine guns and mortars weigh more than rifles. A weapons platoon becomes no more than mules.

> Dear Elliot . . .
> Don't carry anything heavy. Hernia runs in our family, and your Uncle Isadore wore a truss, we later discovered. And for years we thought that dancing made him romantic.

Elliot read me each of his mother's letters. "I love her," he explained. "And I want to share her with a friend. Even if you're a *goy*." He shrugged and then laughed. "So nobody's perfect."

Every week we all received a free ration of beer and chocolate candy. Today I still pop a suds and enjoy chocolates by the box. The taste, in such combination, brings it all back as though it were yesterday and I was soldiering again with Elliot.

He was killed.

The Jugs used to string thin unseen wires across the rocky roads. All of our jeeps had wire cutters, like giant beer-can openers, uprightly welded to every front bumper. Except one jeep. Private Elliot Leftowitz was decapitated. I'm grateful I didn't see it happen.

Somewhere in New York City there's a modest neighborhood of grit-caked brownstones or brick tenements, once the home of the best buddy any G.I. could have.

My buddy.

His soul now rests beyond the clouds.

Regardless in which army or under which flag we serve, old soldiers and young soldiers deserve a bunk in Heaven. Because we've already seen Hell. So, for Elliot's sake, I hope there are plenty of pills, Passover macaroons, and a fresh homemade salami.

May he smell a breeze over the Bronx.

# Saw

AT AGE NINETEEN I RECEIVED MY HONORABLE DISCHARGE from the United States Army. And three hundred dollars.

Even during World War II there wasn't much of a war boom in Vermont. If there was, nobody noticed. And after the war, when we veterans were home looking for work, there weren't too many jobs.

I was lucky. If you can call it luck, being hired at a local sawmill. Hours were long and the pay was short. The noise was deafening. The saws were large and powerful. My job was to be a sawyer's helper, doing whatever was asked of me, obeying the older men I worked with, and shying away from the saw blade.

The man who owned the mill was Mr. Ryan.

Even though he had ample money, he was no stranger to hard honest work. He paid in cash, and never once was a penny short. Or a penny over.

Working, he'd outsweat a horse.

He would start early, way before dawn, getting the mill machinery ready for the day's grind. After we left in the evening, Mr. Ryan was still there, cleaning up, sweeping, doing paperwork. But to me he seemed incomplete. The man couldn't smile. He didn't carry a single laugh inside his ribs. Not a one. He lived alone. Mr. Ryan was a widower. No children. Mrs. Ryan, so I'd been told, died before I was born. But for years prior to her death, she never left the house. Kept to home. Aunt Carrie had heard that Mrs. Ryan wasn't right in the head.

Mr. Ryan had no housekeeper. No visitors came. Nor could anyone recall when he'd last attended church, a town meeting, or a village social. Ryan didn't sing or dance, or play any manner of music.

Men at the mill had a private joke about Mr. Ryan's level of laughter: "If Ryan smiled, he'd break his legs."

He knew timber. That much I'll grant him. Ryan was a master sawyer and could set a log into a bin so true that when it final got fed into the blade, the log would yield a maximum of plank, with little waste. Ryan wasn't partial to wasting words or lumber. Use it, save it, wear it, make it do. He'd tallow the leather wheel straps every day—even on Sunday, some claimed, when the mill wasn't running.

My partner was a man named Yaw.

Mr. Earnest Yaw, a sawyer. I'd been to school with one of his eleven children, Calvin. Earnest was considered, even by other lumberjacks, a large man. Burly, barrel-chested, and balder than a round-top grave marker.

A good worker, tough and knowing. He was Ryan's type of man: taut, tireless, and taciturn. On the rare occasions that Earnest spoke to me above the noise of the saw, I listened up.

Bull-strong, he'd strip off his shirt and then shoulder even the thickest log into the feeder bin, with little help from me. Even though, at the time, I measured six foot high and two hundred pounds of cement. It was admirable the way Earnest Yaw could work. He'd use a wood hook better than a hand, to prick the bark just deep enough to take a purchase on a log and hold weight. Neither too shallow nor too deep.

Yaw wasn't perfect.

He brought whiskey in his dinner pail.

If Ryan knew, he never mentioned it. Perhaps he didn't know. I could never smell liquor on Earnest Yaw's breath. For good reason. Following every swig, Earnest took a bite out of a large raw onion.

The other men kidded him about it in a good-natured way, telling Earnest that his breath, if directed upward, could salt a heavy rain, or kill crows.

Work in a sawmill is always the same. Our days went by, log after log and hour after hour, until the quit whistle blew. Every shift seemed identical to yesterday's. Except for one particular day. It was a Monday, and Earnest Yaw refused to touch his noon meal, claiming his stomach had been turned.

All day long, however, he drank.

With no food in his belly to absorb the colorless corn, Yaw became roaring drunk, cursing the logs that we were hooking into the bin. His wood hook slipped a few times. Earnest moved unsteady. His big boots kicked things they ordinarily would avoid. He didn't bother with eating an onion. Swallow by swallow, the whiskey began to warp him, twisting his body and reason into a half ox and half devil. Yaw had gone and Satan had come.

His eyes became two burning red Hells.

The giant silver circle of the saw cried extra loud that afternoon. A woman's scream. I could hear her pain every time the blade bit into another crooked log. Twice the saw bucked. The blade's cry climbed in pitch, higher, more frantic. The sound of a sick or a wounded animal, as if the mill had been cursed. And was dying.

Oak.

We worked oak that day. I know because even now I can close my eyes and smell it. Hard, like the wood. Many a log, settled improperly in the bin, would balk at the blade, hissing, spitting knots like shotgun balls. A lot of good oak ruined, fouled by temper. Even when a log was beyond correction, Yaw would swear, shouldering the log to push it. Yet the planks we were cutting weren't worthy.

Yaw's answer was to turn up the power until the arrow pointed to a speed beyond safety. In the red of the dial.

He was working closer to the blur of that whirling blade than any man ought.

"Earnest," I said, "please take care."

A man like Earnest Yaw rarely, if ever, hearkens to a boy of nineteen. He was in no mood for advice. Not from a lad young enough to be his son. Ignoring me, he stretched his wood hook across a butted end, his dusty arm between the log and the blade. He trued the log. But it rolled, pinning his arm beneath its massive moving weight.

Dropping my hook, I leaped for the switch just as Mr. Ryan arrived.

In less than a second, Ryan threw his body at the log, knowing that the emergency switch could never cut the power in time. Mr. Ryan and I moved the log just enough to free up Earnest Yaw's arm from underneath. But as Ryan yanked the arm up, he lost his own hand against the slowing blade.

I saw the silver circle painted red all around with specks of blood. The saw blade wore a red belt.

A pair of heavy iron tongs hung on a nail in the nearby wall.

Grabbing them in an instant, Earnest applied them to Ryan's arm to stem the gushering blood. But the sawdust floor was darkening, a blacker and deeper red. The separated hand was draining white. Yaw's fingers gently picked bloody grains of sawdust from the butt of Mr. Ryan's arm. Then, striking a match with his thumbnail, he lit a torch to cauterize the wound. By the time, however, that he'd bound it tight with string, Ryan was breathing irregular and hard.

He fainted on the sawdust floor.

Later on, Doc Turner said that Mr. Ryan might've bled to death, but he lived. Yaw and I left Doc Turner's place and returned to work the mill. There was no such thing as a spoken "Thank you" by either party. No one said a word.

Earnest Yaw never touched another drink.

# Buck Dillard

"HOLD HER STEADY," SAID BUCK.

A crowd had gathered to watch.

Nobody I knew had ever seen it done, what we were about to see, but if anybody was strong enough to actual do such a trick, it was Buck Dillard.

Mr. Dillard was easy to identify. There couldn't have been two lumberjacks like Buck, even though he appeared to be almost two people. He measured six and a half foot in height and weighed close to three hundred pounds. Across one side of his face ran a wood-hook scar. His right hand was slightly crippled from when it had been crushed beneath a log. A double-bitted ax usual hung from his belt.

Some local citizens (especially those who worked, drank, and fought with him) said there was little good in Buck.

Others claimed none at all.

Years ago, when a boy, I had seen Buck Dillard but never dared to speak to him. Few did. Now I was nineteen, home from my military service and working for Mr. Ryan at his sawmill. Buck showed up there once in a while, bringing logs. I still didn't say a how-do to him, nor he to me.

Buck and his wood cords weren't cordial. But we all had to credit Buck Dillard because whenever he was only half drunk, he could entertain a crowd of fire hydrants. Or even preachers.

"Hold her," Buck said again.

With his big logger boots near to a yard apart, Buck bent himself down to position his shoulders underneath Mildred, the mule. She kicked, but didn't hurt Buck any. Hooking a mighty arm around a foreleg, his other around a hind, Buck now locked Mildred into a no-struggle hold.

Buck grunted.

Yet nothing happened.

Behind me, I heard another wager being agreed on, in polite whispers. A bet of five dollars against ten that Buck could heft up a full-growed mule.

Buck's face was normally a ruddy color, a result of outdoor logging in northern Vermont's wind and bitter cold. Now, as he strained, his cheeks reddened to the shade of an embarrassed beet. Mildred still refused to defy gravity.

I heard Buck say a shameful word.

Hauling in a deep breath, Buck strained again. This time, all four hoofs lifted up off the ground. Inch by inch, Buck's tree-trunk legs began to straighten, and Mildred became elevated to free and clear. Knees locked, Buck stood up tall and proud, turning a complete circle, possibly to allow Mildred a good look at a crowd of doubters. She seemed unimpressed.

Everybody made some sort of a noise: a sigh of relief or a groan of disappointment, depending on how a person had wagered.

Mildred brayed, a sound that sawed through the air, so Buck set her gently down and then gave her a hug and a pat. Buck Dillard wasn't a man who'd smile every decade, but he certain was doing it now. All it did was make his scar appear to be deeper, meaner, and more painful.

His real name wasn't Buck.

It was Maurice.

Buck didn't favor his given name, not from a neighbor or a stranger. Just hearing "Maurice" seemed to sour his soul. And double his good fist. In fact, there was only one citizen in the entire county that ever called him Maurice and survived it. She was my teacher, Miss Kelly, the smallest and most birdlike little lady in our community.

There was a rumor that persisted about those

two. Seems that Buck and some other loggers were in town one evening to sign on with a new timber company to skid rough spruce down off the mountain to the pulp mill. All the men signed the work docket except for one. Buck didn't know how to sign his name.

So he didn't get hired.

That was the very night, so the story goes, he pounded on Miss Kelly's door, apologized, then begged her to teach him how to use his left hand to write his name.

Maurice Dillard.

He'd balked at writing the Maurice part, so Miss Kelly told him that signing on as M. Dillard would do. And if this proved inadequate, she personally would speak to the company foreman on Buck's behalf.

Buck, fortified by his newly acquired talent (plus a few swallows from a jug), signed the docket the very next morning when the crew was being assembled. With a bit less ease than he'd lifted the mule, using his good left hand, he picked up the pencil stub, wet the lead tip in his mouth, made a few warm-up circles to be fancy, and signed:

*M. Dillard*

It took him over a minute, but Buck completed

his scrawl, slapping the pencil down with tri-umphant finality.

The foreman, a stranger in these parts, eyed Buck's messy signature and then promptly made a major mistake. "What's the *M* stand for?" he asked.

"Mildred," hooted a lumberjack, a fellow of wit and the brains of a Chiclet.

Several others laughed.

So, a fight broke out. Needless to say, Buck Dillard started it, finished it, and enjoyed every punch and kick from beginning to end. By the time the dust cleared, the docket of able-bodied workers got shortened by several names. To make matters worse, the company paymaster couldn't hear (or think) too well, and Buck's first paycheck was made out to Mildred Dillard.

All the paychecks were cut at the company headquarters. It was corporate policy to print in a first name as well as a last. As a result, there ensued a week-after-week brawl on paydays, with Buck playing a major role.

It took Miss Kelly to straighten it all out by writ-ing an explanatory letter to the company. Future checks were issued to M. Buck Dillard.

Peace was restored. Buck promised Miss Kelly that he'd ease up on drinking and try water. Surpris-ingly, he did.

From then on, a cleaned-and-dressed capon

ready to stuff and roast got delivered personally to Miss Kelly every Christmas by a very beefy delivery boy. When she died, the same giant of a man carried her coffin in his arms, as easy as a child would tote a favorite rag doll inside a shoe box. I was there and saw it all.

The scar on his face was wet and shining, but inside Buck Dillard perhaps a deeper scar had healed.

# Paper

MILLS.

You name almost any kind of a mill and I can tell you, in detail, what working in such a place is like.

If you ever go touring in Vermont or the Adirondacks and arrive at a certain town where most of the menfolks (and even some of the women) are missing fingers, you can wager you're in a paper mill town. Now I can't say for sure that a paper mill is the worst place on earth to work, but it has just got to be rotten close. Especially if it's some old relic of a man-killer that should have been torn to the ground half a century ago.

In a paper mill, there are massive machines, chemicals, steam, and the dispositions of some of the foremen, whose lives are every mite as miserable as those of us in the crews.

A paper mill is noise, wet, heat, danger.

Add to this the raw reality that there's no chance to escape. For almost all of the men and women, it's a way of life. And, to paraphrase the *Porgy and Bess* ballad, the living *ain't* easy.

Let's presume that you are intelligent and, if so, you have an inquiring mind. Then you are in for an industrial treat to visit a papermaking mill, take the guided tour that almost any congenial management will offer, and walk through the place. One end to the other.

Paper is basically two things. Wood and water.

I know the papermaking process because, as a lad, I cut my teeth on a Warren Winder. Personally, I have filled every job you can name in an old-fashioned paper mill, from woodhook to freight gang. I have unloaded soda ash in the chemical mill and helped to handle the raw clay. They gave us respirators to cover our noses and mouths, but they weren't worth a hoot. We inhaled the white dust with every breath. Slow death. Coal miners die from black lung. Our lungs were dying white.

Ask any worker who's survived a paper mill about lancing a digester in the chemical mill, the section of the mill that prepares raw wood pulp to become eventual paper. I worked digesters all summer one time. My work partner was a man whose name was Gates. In his day he had been an excellent athlete.

In his day.

By the time he turned thirty, he appeared middle-aged. At forty, old.

Unloading soda ash or clay and stoking a digester (a cooker that reduces tiny pieces of wood to loose fibers) are not the worst mill jobs.

The worst is the chipper room.

Logs arrive, usually by railroad but often locally by truck, and are unloaded by woodhooks (a nickname for mill lumbermen) onto conveyor belts, and then into barkers. There are two kinds: a stream barker fires jets of water with incredible pressure to peel off the bark; a drum barker is a slowly rotating cylinder, ten or twelve feet in diameter, through which the loose logs are sent, pounded, and relieved of their hide.

From there to a chipper room.

One by one, the chipper-room operator must feed large logs (weighing sometimes hundreds of pounds) into the chipper blades, which are capable of reducing these spruce monsters into wood fragments the size of a poker chip.

In seconds.

The noise is intense.

There's only one noise comparable, that of a severe Florida hurricane.

Chipper-room noise has a way of beating and pounding and hammering a man into submission, robbing him of awareness. Finally he tunes out, hearing only the chipper. In a few years he will hear nothing at all, not even the voices of his wife and his children.

Paper mills shut down only on Sunday. During the six-day week, they run all day and all night. On shifts. If your relief man doesn't show up (a lot don't), you are, by union rule, obligated to remain on the job for a second shift.

This is necessary. The mill has to run.

But after hours and hours of deafening chipper-room noise, during which you actually do become deaf in self-defense, the extra shift leaves you an unfeeling, uncaring, unhearing mute. After work, the chippers would sit outside on a bench, saying nothing. We were a row of warm corpses. Our children could have been slaughtered before our eyes and our reactions might have been non-existent.

We were men turned wooden.

Like the chips.

Every working day, a paper mill runs twenty-four hours. Today that means three eight-hour shifts. But years ago it was only two. The day tour was eleven hours, and the night crew worked thirteen. There were no rest periods. The paper machines that produced the finished product in huge rolls never stopped; we ate whenever we could grab a bite of a sandwich, on the job, in this mayhem of manufacturing, where only a demon without a soul could survive.

My co-workers were mostly decent guys.

Many of the foremen were good too. And the machine runners (senior types) were dedicated papermakers, honest professionals who would rip a swatch of paper off a roll, hold it up to a light box in the testing laboratory, and marvel that they'd produced one beautiful sheet of paper on equipment that deserved to be retired half a century ago.

When there, I got plenty of good advice from the old mill hands and woodhooks. "Now's the time," they said. "While you're young, get out of here, boy. Scoot yourself away while you're able and you still have ten fingers. Don't spend no lifetime in a dang paper mill. It'll own ya. It will eventual rob a soul."

While dispensing such worthy guidance, the longtimers pointed at me with hands that were missing fingers. So few hands were complete.

Winter came. All during the winter months we worked inside, in temperatures above one hundred degrees. Way above.

Then, when the shift whistle blew (if your relief

man came), you escaped from the heat to walk home in sub-zero weather. It was enough to cause a man to cuss if his partner's truck wouldn't start. Get home, wash, eat, sleep, and then travel back to the paper mill for the next shift.

Somehow we did it.

No one had to inform us that we were *men*.

Sometimes at night when I was too tired to sleep, I'd lie awake, my mind composing poetry. Not fancy or fine. Yet I sort of wanted the world to know how it was, the way we lived, worked, wasted, and died.

I wrote me a poem:

PAPER MILL

Winter wind sinks mercury
To zero. But inside
A paper mill, the temperature
Can nearly roast your hide.

Night-shift men on hungry
Boilers fire steam. And when
The viper hiss comes up, you believe
You'll never breathe again.

Mill machines are starving. Mean
Enough to take their toll

Of men. And try to boil your heart—
Before they cook your soul.

Paper men. We wear our soaking
Rags about the place.
Old in body. Old in mind.
And older in the face.

Our hands are missing fingers and
Our hands are missing thumbs.
Some hands are just enough to hold
The coffee. If it comes.

We're demon men. Our backs are soaked
In work. We have no will,
Only resignation that
We can't escape the mill.

Paper mills are foul holes,
The darkest of the caves.
Machines are lashing masters and
They truly beat their slaves.

Watch! When winter morning steams
The ground, and know full well . . .
That Satan is our foreman
In the paper mill of Hell.

# Dr. Granberry

THE TIMBER COMPANY THREW US A PICNIC.

On a summer Sunday in 1949, beside a mountain lake, scores of us lumberjacks and woodhooks assembled to eat, get drunk, fall off a rolling log into icy water, cuss, fistfight, and throw axes at trees. Or at each other. Some would duel with chain saws.

Yet intellectually, a day that changed my life.

A stranger came.

Few knew or cared why this gentleman appeared. He was a football scout for small colleges, looking for linemen and recruiting mindless brutes. Naturally he spotted me, very young and weighing 230. My shoulder-length hair was blacker than a crow's wing and held in place by a single lace of rawhide. After the stranger told me his name, we shook hands. No one else bothered to greet him, but I was younger and more curious.

When he asked me if I ever considered going away to a college, I told him no. College was for the sons of wealthy men. My pa had butchered hogs.

Scholarship money, the stranger informed me, was scarce. But, as a war veteran, I might apply for funds under the G.I. Bill and be educated. Perhaps even graduate. Following that Sunday, I never saw or heard from him again. Before leaving the picnic, however, he gave me a document to be filled out, signed, notarized, and mailed. I asked what it was. Prior to answering, he glanced around at all of my brawling, swearing, puking companions.

"It's your ticket out of the sewer."

Weeks later, a thousand miles from home, wearing my new nineteen-dollar suit from the Wultex factory in Troy, New York, I had enrolled. The suit was the only one in my size. Wultex didn't carry many suits in a 50 long.

You could call it my Going Away Suit because so many people looked at me, flinched, and said, "Go away."

Nonetheless, I was a college student. But I enjoyed no social life. No dates, even though many of the coeds looked so pretty. So clean. Like new pennies. Sometimes, from behind the protection of all of my hair, I secretly stared at them. My suit amused them even though I wore it every day. A black-and-white salt-and-pepper tweed with subtle red flecks. Stiffer than burlap.

Nobody else had a suit like it. At least not in Florida during a steaming September.

All I did was sleep, eat, go to football practice, and then limp home to a shower, supper, the library, and into bed at ten o'clock. Next to no one knew my name. Needless to add, I faithfully attended all of my classes, although the subjects assigned to us were so easy. New football boys took a lot of courses together.

They called us Baby Beef.

In town, I met a friendly guy whose name was Granberry, a free spirit like me, and we started hunting for snakes together. It felt good to spend time with him; in a swamp, I didn't wear my suit. Just old Army pants and combat boots. Bless him, he accepted me for what I was.

Late at night, whenever my aching body was so bruised that the pain prevented sleep, I *wrote*. Mostly about snakes, critters, the people back up north in Vermont, kin, folks I missed. Farm animals. A few favorite hymns. And the smells of Mama's kitchen. Even spring manure that turned brown to green: one has to be farm-raised to appreciate the awakening fragrance of fertilizer.

When I read one of my pieces to Granberry, the one about a yellow rat snake that he and I kept around for a pet, I received quite a shock.

"Let my father read it," he told me.

"Who's he? A snake charmer?"

"Oh, he's sort of famous. He writes the *Buzz Sawyer* comic strip and teaches classes in creative writing at the college."

"Here?"

"Yep. Go see Dr. Edwin Granberry. He's a little ol' bald-headed geezer, sort of looks like a buzzard, but plenty okay. You'll like him. Everyone does."

So, wearing a leather thong around my hair, my abrasive suit, my only necktie (also out of the Army), I rapped on Dr. Granberry's door in Orlando Hall. He smiled, said he'd heard about me from his son, and we shook hands. I stood and scratched my Wultex while he read what I'd written. Read it twice. Finally he peered at me over half-moon glasses and snorted a comment.

"*You* wrote this?"

"Yes, sir, the whole bit. If it's no good, you can blame your son, on account it was his idea I'm here, not mine."

"Why don't you sit down?"

"My knees hurt."

"Football?"

I nodded.

Dr. Granberry made a sour face. "I don't cotton to football. And I never much liked anyone who played it." He smiled up at me like a pixie. "Until now. What else have you written?"

"Poems. A few songs. Most of my regular stuff is about the outdoors because that's all I know."

He grinned. "A professional usually writes about what he knows. Nothing else. So you're off to a roaring good start." He stood. "What courses are you into?"

I told him, and again he frowned, yet his eyes narrowed as though in deep professorial cogitation. "Would you please do *us* a favor?" he asked.

"Sure. Glad to, sir."

"There are tests I want you to take. An entire battery they give up in DeLand, at Stetson University. Do you have means of getting there? Any transportation?"

With a grin, I hoisted my thumb. "I'll hitch."

"No you won't. I'll carry you in my car. We'll first arrange a time. These exams will tell me what I want to know about you. Not academic. More for mental agility and capacity. One can't really *study* for them."

"Tough?"

"Not for those with brains." He cracked his cagey little birdlike smile. "I'd bet the farm on you."

After the tests at Stetson, I waited for weeks, didn't hear a word, and presumed I'd flunked. But then I spotted Dr. Granberry waving at me and hollering my name. Excited about something. Yanking me into his tiny paper-littered office, he could hardly speak.

"Robert," he said at last, "what I suspected is now proven. My boy, you're a moth destined to be a butterfly." He held up a manila folder. "I swiped your file from administration. Your schedule." As if in some rapturous rage, he tore my records into pieces. "Goodbye to these mush courses. You're going to take philosophy, psychology, science, logic, math, world history, languages . . . and every single literature and theater course available. Plus a ton of outside reading." He paused for a breather. "Sit down!"

I sat. My knees screamed.

"Robert Newton Peck," he said in a more contained tone, "tell me what you've done in your young life. Right now. But make it brief."

I told him: Farmwork, helped Papa kill hogs. Then a machine gunner overseas. Came home to a sawmill, paper mill, freight gang, and lumber camp. Now a defensive middle guard. Unknown. An unheralded substitute.

Tiny hands reached to cradle my ears and hold my head as though he feared to drop it. "Rob," he said softly, "all your life, people made you into nothing except a beast of burden. They looked at your oxlike frame and thought *ox*. Well, they're all mistaken. You're no mule. From this point on, we're going to employ your *mind*, big fellow, not just your muscles."

"Am I dreaming?"

"No. This is your first icy plunge into reality. Give us four years, my boy, and you won't believe how you've grown by graduation." He squinted. "Must you wear all that black hair so long? If you plan to do much hitchhiking, you'll frighten a motorist right off the road. You look like Geronimo."

For four bits, I bought myself a brush cut.

A number of us had to quit football because of injury. For some reason, my weight dropped by over forty pounds. Coach warned me that if I didn't finish the season, I wouldn't be in the team photograph, or attend the banquet.

I told him that I'd already heard them eat.

Our college discontinued football. Too expensive. Between snake hunting (for profit) and the G.I. Bill, my tuition got paid. I didn't ask the college for a dime. But four years later I wore neither cap nor gown because I had a chance to ride north, for free, a day before commencement. Dean Stone understood after I explained that no one

College senior, on a bench that Papa built.

in my family could afford to come and see me graduate.

He mailed me my diploma in a tube. And it's still inside, rolled up. I never had it framed for an ego wall. Because, for a number of years, I couldn't even afford a wall.

A year at Cornell Law School exhausted every penny of my G.I. Bill, so I escaped to New York City to become a songwriter. Or a comic. I had twenty-four songs published (none famous), plus a few radio jingles, and then stumbled into advertising in 1954.

Except for corporate success, nothing much happened until 1973 and *A Day No Pigs Would Die,* my first novel. Eventually over sixty more, and I'm still writing.

Returning to my alma mater to be honored, I was so pleased that a kind and dedicated Dr. Granberry, who taught me how to write, was there. As he sat beaming in the front row, I couldn't look at him for fear of tears. Needless to say, I mentioned his name, reminding the audience that I'd dedicated a book to him in gratitude. Also one to Dr. Wilbur Dorset. And to Miss Kelly.

Afterward, Dr. Granberry gave me a very special volume from his collection, *The White Goat's Kid,* a short story of gritty determination that bore meaning to us both, and personally signed it:

> To my prize, my treasure,
> Robert Newton Peck.
> I'm so proud of him I cry.

As I bear-hugged the frail little gentleman, we both did.

# Mary

IT WAS LATE.

A few minutes after eight o'clock. Outside my Manhattan corner-office window loomed an inky December night, speckled by thousands of other little windows. Our business day was done. Except for me, all of our employees had hustled home; I was alone at my desk, grooming an advertising proposal for tomorrow morning's client meeting.

Even though my office door was open, I heard a timid knock. Three apologetic taps. Looking up, I saw her.

There was Mary.

That was all I knew concerning her name. Mary, a cleaning lady, hired by the giant office building to police up the dirt, litter, butts, and ashes of slick executives and svelte secretaries.

"Not right now, Mary. Perhaps in about an hour. Please do the other offices and leave mine for last. Okay?"

She never moved.

Looking at her, I saw a tired face and a slumped body, aged beyond her years, no education, dressed in clothes that were close to cleaning cloths. Rags. One stocking had fallen and was collapsed above her shoe. Her entire appearance said *charwoman*.

"Well?" I asked.

There was an object in her hands. Neither a sponge nor a scrub brush. No mop. A second later I recognized an item oddly out of place. A book.

"Mr. Peck, I . . . I gotta ask your help."

"What's up?" I asked, more out of get-it-over-with speed than concern.

"I got a problem."

"Yes?"

Mary took a few steps toward me. "It's about Anthony."

"Who's he?"

"Anthony is my son," she said. "He's going to become an engineer. If he can make it through college. My boy's got a chance."

"Good," I said, without much sincerity.

"Anthony, he's my youngest. I got five. But the older ones won't never amount to nothing. No future. They'll be lucky to end up like me."

She advanced another cautious step.

"What's the book?"

"Algebra. My son calls it math. But I guess it's his weak spot. Comes hard for him. So for years now, I learned to do math too. We learn it together. Me and Anthony."

"Oh?"

"This ain't no beginner algebra. This is the hard stuff. Advanced, he says. I can't understand it no more. My eyesight can't keep up. So maybe my son's going to fail."

Dropping my pencil, I stared at her in a sudden rush of respectful disbelief. Although shocked, I found the strength to speak.

"Mary . . . you are studying *advanced algebra*?"

She nodded, then slowly lifted the algebra textbook as though making a final offering to an altar. To make the bells ring in the chapel of a Christmas fable.

"It's . . . number 74."

I sighed. "Mary, it's late, and I'm very—"

"Please," she begged. "I don't got nobody else to ask. I'm stuck. Went as far as I can go. But unless I understand quadratics, I can't explain it to my boy so he'll graduate and be a *somebody*." Her spine straightened. "An engineer."

I was silent. Mary continued.

"Anthony . . . he's sort of all the hope I got."

"What about your husband? They claim that men are more into mathematics. Could *he* help?"

"Louie died. Took a cough, about ten years back. Doctor bills? You can't believe what it cost me. So all I got to help me is *you*."

There it lay on my big walnut desk, a marketing plan for a new deodorant, one that society needed about as much as I longed for a second navel. At this speed, I wouldn't catch a train to Connecticut and report home at ten o'clock. On a night when I'd promised my wife I'd help put up the Christmas tree. Family was coming tomorrow. But a spruce would have to wait.

"May I look at the problem?"

"Sure. You have a lot of brains. It'll be a cinch for somebody like you, Mr. Peck. You got education. I don't."

Mary's assessment of my mathematical talents was far beyond coping, I feared. Because I was another Anthony. Math was murder, and I had been a perpetual victim. Gary Blake, one of my competent assistants, served as my numbers guy. Details. Stats. Figures on a sheet of paper danced for Gary. Why wasn't he here when I needed him? Home, I mused, putting up *his* tree. The rat.

"Let me take a squint, Mary."

She gave me the open book. *Advanced Algebra.* The equations seemed to be written in Japanese italics. Flipping back a few pages, I reinforced what little I knew with regard to solving quadratic equations. I mumbled the formula as I read: "$X$ equals $A$ minus $B$, plus or minus the square root of $B$ squared minus $4AC$ over $2A$."

It seemed to be a guideline to finding the value of an unknown $X$ when given the three other values as constants. Armed with my brief refresher, I jumped ahead to problem 74. Into the valley of Death rode the six hundred. Or, to be more appropriate, the Lone Ranger.

Glancing at my desk phone, I had the urge to call Gary Blake and order him to haul his freight over to Mary's house to tutor Anthony. Gary would have to drop his tinsel and hustle out into a wintry night and perform his math magic for the fifth child of a scrubwoman.

Call it Christmas. Label it anything you please. Like lunacy. There's no logical explanation why I, the math moron, boned over an algebra problem. It was Greek. Yet desperation has a talent for knighting a serf into a scholar. It was amazing how much Mary (I didn't even know her family name) had mastered of the finer points of factoring, even when so many values were parenthetical and, if you'll allow, problematic.

Perhaps, right around Christmastime, an algebraic angel beams down to tap a confused shoulder, to enlighten, to inspire with a competence beyond deserving.

Mary and I did it!

A merry miracle.

Christmas, so it goes, is a time for gift giving. The gift I received that night, sweating over numerical values far beyond me (and cursing the ghost of John Napier), was later valued above any price I paid. Sometimes the most I can give is the least I have, yet everything that a Christmas spirit could inspire. I made a bell ring. Not a cathedral carillon. Merely a tiny tinkle from the curled-up toe of Santa's elf.

Never did I know whether or not Anthony graduated from college. Let's fervently hope so. Perhaps because his mother's name is Mary, as was the name of the woman who lived two thousand years ago, a Mary birthing a son who didn't become an engineer.

Only a carpenter.

# Wings

In Vermont there were Pecks aplenty. Uncle Charles sired fourteen children, Uncle Edward begot ten, and my father, Haven, added seven more. As seventh, I was the runt among thirty-one.

Townsfolk called us "uproaders," an unflattering label for those have-nots who resided in gray unpainted shacks, along dirt roads instead of pavement. We called *them* "downhillers." Perhaps in envy of their rich bottom land (compared to our rocks and stumps), indoor plumbing, electricity, and store-bought clothes.

Although poor, my parents convinced me that we were comfortable off. More important, hearty harvests had blessed us with a bounty for which anyone ought to bow thankful. "Gratefulness," my mother fervently insisted, "is our highest note in the hymn of prayer."

Miss Lucy, as Papa so often called my mother, was a model of compromise. Merchandise we couldn't afford she branded as "a frill," a luxury no God-fearing Shaker would covet. Once a week I was informed that Divine Benevolence had again beamed down upon us and our table.

We ate chicken every Sunday.

Our daily trio of meals was referred to as breakfast, dinner, and supper. Lunch was whatever a kid toted to school for a noon repast . . . in a *dinner* pail. I doubt that today's students, seated in their million-dollar cafeterias, have the fun we enjoyed. How? Trading sandwiches! My sandwich was often a thick layer of pork-flavored baked beans between two slabs of homemade brown bread. Ah, but a noontime Sunday dinner was an event, due to the fact, I presumed, that fowl provided more sanctity than jowl.

Guests, ever present, were served first crack at the chicken. White meat. Breast. We youngsters made do with the darker thighs and drumsticks.

Mama always ate a wing.

No amount of persuasion could make her do otherwise, not even after I'd become a grown man, married, seated at her table with my wife, son Christopher, and daughter Anne. My mother ate one chicken wing while Aunt Carrie dutifully gnawed the other. Younger generations dared not dispute Vermont virtue. A man's naught but a simpleton if he challenges the New England rigidity of his elders and betters.

In countless ways, Miss Lucy and Miss Carrie were softer than winter bed quilts. Yet by necessity, granite-hard.

They were sisters who lived their entire lives together under one roof, pulling more willingly than a yoke of Holstein oxen. Aunt Carrie was seven years older, and as time took a toll on her teeth, she eventual yielded to partake of the more pliant breast meat. But it took my mother's influence to break the established pattern.

Years earlier, I'd attempted the impossible by slyly helping myself to both wings, claiming they contained a certain nutrient to improve my (you name it) eyesight, hearing, or virility.

No dice.

The chicken wings were snatched, or eased, from my dinner plate and replaced by generous slabs and slices that appeared whiter than Queen Elizabeth's bosom.

Following Papa's death when I was thirteen, Mama's make-do resolve was made clear to me. Tough times had become even tougher, and the three of us feared losing our little five-acre farm. At mealtime, less and less food graced the kitchen table. Papa's empty chair completed our emptiness.

Added to this, my plate somehow held more supper than my mother's or my aunt's.

We lost our farm to the bank.

On a gray December day, a chilling and merciless north wind seemed to snap our spines as though we were three dead twigs. Mama, Aunt Carrie, and I loaded a few possessions onto a neighbor's wagon and left our home forever.

Until I reached age seventeen, when I enlisted in the United States Army out of desperation and the assurance there'd be money to mail home, Mama saw that I was fed.

Truly a miracle she survived long enough to comprehend that I'd made my mark and become an author.

About to deliver a speech out west, in the state of Washington, I called home only to learn of Mama's death: 7 October 1976. Oddly, it was the most humorous talk I ever gave, maybe because it was all for her. A secret tribute. Someone drove me to the Sea-Tac airport, and I flew from there to San Francisco and took a red-eye to New York, where my driver carried me home to Connecticut.

Unwashed, I changed suitcases and drove myself north almost three hundred miles to a tiny Yankee town, arriving barely in time for Mama's wake.

Silently waiting stood a score of elderly people,

almost all farmers, staring as I charged irreverently through the funeral parlor door. Eyes that met mine spoke more respect for her than for me. Hands that held my hands had been thickened by a lifetime of labor. I was too spent to recall everyone's name.

There she lay, hands still a shiny red from decades at a sink, ringless fingers folded, wearing a very plain dress and looking like someone's sugar-haired mom. Mine. Touching her a final time, I remembered how a mother rises upward and into Heaven.

On the wings of a chicken.

# Part III
# Florida Years

# Ed's Jewel

He was up to something. But what?

As I was well hidden in a generous patch of Florida brush, I could watch this man's unusual activity.

Spying wasn't my intent.

Learning was.

Hours ago and a mile behind, I'd parked a battered Ford pickup under the high shade of a large live oak. Nowhere near a road. Just a stretch of open Florida outback, griddle-flat and griddle-hot. All I toted was a pistol at my right hip, binoculars, a canteen half filled with spring water that was, probable by now, warmer than I was, plus a pocket notepad and three or four stubby golf pencils.

Moving in closer to take a more intimate look, I now estimated the man's age on the far side of seventy, twenty years my senior. His hair seemed to be

Up aboard Old Soup. Florida, 1977.

a wet silver. He was barefoot. No shirt. I'd make a considered guess that he was wearing only a single article of clothing. A bib overall. No longer denim blue but a washboard gray, ragged at the bottom. Knees worn to white. Ditto the two straps that hung on thin shoulders.

Using a two-foot stick, he stirred the contents of a keg in circles, sometimes thumping the inside wood. Bending, he looked inside the keg and nodded.

Leaving my shelter, I circled to where I could easily walk directly toward his face and not creep up from behind to startle him. "Howdy," I said, waving a hand.

Either he didn't hear or didn't care to, so I advanced closer and spoke louder.

This time he looked up, squinted, then put down his mixer wand to shade his eyes. He probable noticed my sidearm in its holster, yet he didn't retreat an inch. Or flinch.

"Hot day," I told him.

His nod agreed.

Coming to within twenty-five feet of him, I stopped, then unscrewed the black cap of my canteen. Before drinking even a sip, I held the olive-drab-covered U.S. Army canteen toward him, making sure to use my right hand. My left couldn't draw a gun.

"Thirsty?" I asked as I smiled.

He shook his head.

I drank a warm swallow.

"You the law?"

"No. I write books."

For a minute he held silent. Poking his stick inside the keg, he stirred three times around, then quit to study at me. "Nope," he said, "you ain't the law."

"How can you tell?"

He spat. "You've no belly." It didn't make a smart of sense to ask questions about what he was mixing in the wooden keg. None of my business. After knocking back another shot of warm water, I twisted the cap back on and rehung the canteen to my belt. Left hip.

His eyes watched my hands. "Your water's cooking," he guessed.

"Sure is."

"There's a boil yonder. Cool water. You happen to know exact what a boil is? Or are you city?"

I knew. "Yes, it's a very young spring. You'll find a boiler in a forest, at a quiet place, among trees. Usual in shallow water, indicating that someday a spring might be gushering up there." I shrugged. "That's all I know."

There were questions I wanted to pose to this old gentleman, but didn't. So far, all I'd asked was whether or not he was thirsty, a gesture more courteous than probing. Right now I was on his turf. The nearer an animal to its nest or lair, the tougher it'll scrap. So I wasn't fixing to crowd him or inquire more, figuring that the early questions rightfully ought to be his.

"Well, if you come around here-parts to sell me a book, you're wasting air."

Perhaps, in his way, he was implying that he couldn't read, without actually confessing.

"I knowed somebody was nearby," he said. "The dog whined to tell me. You been here a spell."

Glancing about, I saw no dog.

"She be lame. But her nose ain't. She's to the shack, guarding our dooryard. Don't walk too good no more. Gimpy-legged. Can't see neither. But smell? She'll scent a bug through a bunghole." He pointed back toward a stand of pine. "From yonder, she smelt *you*."

His pride made me like him. An aging man proud of an aging dog. In a way, he was bragging about her.

"She's a redbone." He sighed. "Lordy knows, I don't got me a whole bit to boast, but she be the best hunter hound that ever treed a coon, or tracked a possum."

"I'd like to meet her."

"Already she's met up you." Straining, the old fellow tried to heft up the keg, and failed. "Dang," he said, "it's too much."

Slowly, I approached him. "Just maybe the two of us might handle it. Where's it go?"

"Over yonder."

As I'm six foot four and well over two hundred pounds, farm-raised and iron-pumped, I could have easily hoisted the keg to a shoulder. But there was no reason to show off to shame him. Seniors deserve respect. Together, we lifted it. I let him steer.

"Here," he said.

After we grounded the keg and tilted it, dumping the mysterious elixir into a blanket of brown pine needles, he sprinkled a few needles over the lumpy mess to mask it.

Straightening up, he said, "They'll come smell."

"Who?"

"Young tuskers."

"If a tusker comes, do you try to capture it?"

To my surprise, he shook his head.

"He'll be prowling. He eats and he goes. But ever time, I dump the acorn mash closer to my pen. Eat and go. Eat some more. But final, he'll eat free mash and tarry. Then me and my hound'll both chomp on pork."

A tusker is a wild Florida pig. I'd seen plenty. No animal on earth is tougher, or more ornery. Even armed with a pistol, I wouldn't want to face one. Some mature boars balance over five hundred pound. If you doubt, read *Nine Man Tree*.

"I'll tame 'em," he said.

I had to ask a short question: "How?"

Lifting the empty keg, he said, "It's sour corny mash laced with acorns. A pig can't pass it by. They'll turn lazy on free found. So shiftless and fatbacked they'll not root for theyselves no longer. I git 'em so dumb they'll depend to me. Once they do, they're bacon.

"Pigs think it's charity," he added. "Ain't. It's volunteer slavery."

Extending a hand to him, I said, "My name is Peck. Friends call me Rob."

We shook. His hand was harder than a gator claw, hooking around mine with a surprising strength.

"Nocker. Ed Nocker."

"A pleasure to meet you, Mr. Nocker."

"Yeah," he said, "it sure is." He cracked his first grin. "You want to greet my bitch?"

"If it's okay with her."

As we walked, Mr. Nocker carried the empty keg above his hip, on its side. The weight of his arm seemed to tote it suspended, without any hand to hold it. His walk was unsteady, as though every step was arthritic agony. Sometimes he would moan. Or grunt.

Into the pines, we came to a small gray shack in a clearing, behind a prone dog.

"Jewel. Her name is Jewel."

The redbone hound was lying in a tiny cloud of shade. Raising her chin from her paws, ears up, she stared at us through the snowy eyes of wintry blindness, nostrils flaring, thirsting for information. At the mention of her name, a tail wagged once and then stilled.

"Best you don't touch her," he warned. "Unless

you intend to give up picking a banjo."

"I won't."

"Later, she'll up herself and stretch for a while. Then allow her to come to you. After she does, you can love her and scratch her neck to all content." Mr. Nocker bent to stroke her head. "Good dog. We got company, Jewel. So favor us a mite with manners. Hear?"

He went inside. Mr. Nocker didn't ask me to enter his shack. Just as well, as I doubted that there would be room for two. My eye judged it to be about ten foot square, and even less than a ten-foot cube. A low roof, and flat. Reappearing, he carried a leathery object, one that seemed to be under construction, yet solidly built.

"It's near finish."

He handed it to me. Taking it, I was surprised at its mass. Hefty. But sturdy and artistically crafted. Quite smooth. Some leather is so cold. This was cozy.

"Mule collar," he told me.

"You keep a mule?"

He didn't answer. Perhaps because my question was, in retrospect, more than a bit silly. Why else would he be fashioning a mule's tack? Certainly not for Jewel.

Mr. Nocker cooked.

We ate outdoors on a bench. Controlling both

caution and curiosity, I gagged down what he served me, chewing it with gritted teeth, swallowing as my craw earned a medal for valor. Scraping the bent tin plate with my fork, I thanked him.

"Good supper," I said, raking a sleeve across my mouth and waiting for Ed to explain, after the fact, our menu.

He didn't. But from the taste still haunting my mouth, I guessed possum. This, I decided, was real research, the kind that no author could uncover in a library, absorbed not into the brain but down the gullet.

Jewel came.

To her, perhaps, there was no difference between day or night. All was darkness. Mr. Nocker fed her a few scraps from the black cooking pot that had prepared our meal. He chewed for her, offering her half-gnawed chunks of meat from his mouth to hers, allowing her to smell, then swallow. "Her teeth are most missing," he explained. Her body was leaner than a dry-spell bean. A rib counter. One of her back feet was missing, snubbed off at the first joint, so I asked how it had happened.

"Gator."

Jewel, I noticed, was beyond feeble. Lame to almost halt. And blind. When, at last, Jewel did stagger over to investigate me, and then accept me, I rubbed and petted her for a time. Then she flopped down as if in considerable pain, and stared at me with her frozen eyes.

"If Jewel will pardon us," Mr. Nocker said, "let's go around back."

We went.

He pointed out two graves: one large, the other small and empty. The large grave was merely a mound of grassless and weedless red sand.

"Esme," he said, "is buried here."

"I'm sorry."

"We lived together better'n thirty year. She pulled her weight, Esme did. Never once had to lick a stick to her."

My face puzzled at him. Perhaps he was joking. Although it was possible that a hermit such as Ed Nocker could get away with wife beating, as there were no neighbors to hear her screams.

He sudden laughed.

"You know," he said softly, "I teached Esme how to shake hands. People'd stop by, years back, to see her do it. Esme was stubborn. She'd only shake with me. Not nobody else. A stranger wouldn't have the luck of a gigged bullfrog. He'd just stand there, looking fooly, with his hand out and fingers open, but Esme wouldn't offer."

"Why not?"

"Can't say. Stubborn. But I'd still have to credit Esme. She was a worthy mule."

*Mule?*

Before I could speak, or even stutter, Mr. Nocker pointed at the other grave, the smaller one, recently dug, as the fresher and darker earth indicated.

"I can't do it," he said.

"Do what?"

"Mister . . . forgit your name . . . don't guess I can perform what I ought . . . for Jewel."

"This grave is for her?"

He nodded. "You pack a pistol," he said. It sounded more as a question than a statement. "I ain't going to pretend I can handle it, because the Lord didn't built me strong enough." Turning, he faced the sunset with his back to me. "You probable think I'm a sorry old fool."

"No I don't."

"Well, you got cause. Here I be, trying to finish making a work collar for a dead mule. I got reason. Years back, her old collar got wore to sorry, so I promised Esme I'd fashion her 'nother."

I wondered what I should do. Thank Mr. Nocker for my supper, tell him that I didn't have any cartridges in the pistol, and leave?

Such would prove me a coward.

"Jewel's in torment," he said. "In the night, she tries to roll or git up, and the stiff makes her howl. It ain't a hunting bugle. That I recall. It's her death wail. She's begging me to let her go home. Only reason I chew her food to keep her alive is because Jewel needs me. Esme don't need me no more. Nobody do. It's a crime for me to keep Jewel alive for so flimsy a reason. Ought to hang my head."

I swallowed. "All right," I told him.

"You'll do her?"

"Yes." I stood. "Mr. Nocker, do you want me to carry her to where you've dug her grave?"

He shook his head. "No. She mine and I'm hers. It'll be the final thing I can perform for her. Our last walk together. I'll burden her in a bit, after we say so long."

I waited.

Mr. Nocker came, carrying Jewel, his unburied treasure. He walked slowly, perhaps to feel needed for one extra bonus of time. When my Ruger fired, Mr. Nocker clutched at his own heart, eyes clenched, as though the bullet had torn through him as well. He buried her. I offered to help but he wouldn't allow. As I left, he took my hand. His palm was gritty with sand from the grave of a dead hound named Jewel. I had a hunch he wouldn't soap it off.

"Thanks," he whispered.

"I hope you finish Esme's collar."

"Oh, I will. I got it planned."

"You have enough leather?"

Ed nodded. "Yes, and just enough days."

# Charlie Moon Sky

I OWN A SPECIAL KNIFE.

Charlie Moon Sky, a very senior Florida Seminole, made the knife for me. And to honor him and his tribe (providing they destroy no more panthers to prove their manhood), his knife will ride my leg.

During my lifetime, I have collected few trophies. They can be counted on the fingers of one hand:

> Infantry badge, WWII
> Chief of the Indian Guides
> Mark Twain Award
> Senior Games gold medal
> One Seminole knife

Believe it or doubt it, I wouldn't barter away any of the above in order to accept a Pulitzer or the

Nobel. What little I have, I'll keep, because all five fit me. Better yet, touching them continues to please. Secret ego trips. Not to be displayed, but tucked away somewhere, in a worn-out saddlebag.

Charlie Moon Sky and I met three decades ago, near a small South Florida town, Immokalee, east of Fort Myers. He knew the Okaloacoochee Slough as though he had planned it for a backyard garden. South of there is a mythical tree, perhaps even sacred, and I suspect a part of Charlie's personal religion. A tall, very thick cypress, one that takes nine men, arms extended to link their fingers into an endless circular chain, to stretch around its great gray trunk.

And its legendary name is Nine Man Tree.

Charlie and I got to meet, and to distrust each other, in a span of minutes. He had just downed a panther. A magnificent female. Worse yet, she appeared to me to have been pregnant.

"Are you ashamed?" I asked him.

He stiffened. "It is a part of my religion," Charlie Moon Sky told me. "A tribal rite. It is a Seminole's right to slay a panther. His heritage."

Facing him square, I said, "Oh, is that so? Well, it just happens to be my religion to kill a Seminole. Unless I do, I won't feel that I'm fully a man; not until I stretch a Seminole hide to dry on the side of my barn."

His eyes blazed.

Yet, for the sake of a beautiful dead animal that had been needlessly slaughtered, I felt like making him squirm. With a bit of a swagger, I informed him that there were panthers in Vermont, and in Canada, much larger than their puny Florida cousins. This is true. "Panthers of this size," I said, sneering at his kill, "are hunted by children, or by old women who are crippled or blind."

He scowled.

But then, following a long pause, it became his turn to sneer. "How large," he asked me, "are the panthers *you* kill?"

Shaking my head, I admitted the truth, that I had tracked them but never successfully. Recently I'd tried finding panthers in a Florida swamp and never saw one. Only scat and paw prints. No cat. I confessed that, between the two of us, he was the better hunter.

In agreement, he nodded slowly.

"This panther," he said quietly, "I stalked and killed with an arrow. One arrow. I don't own a gun. Do you?"

"I own guns, but I don't like killing animals for sport. Only for food. But that was yesterday, back when I was young and my hair hung black to my shoulders."

"You are honest," he said, "for a white man."

It was time to play my *ace*. So, I informed him that my grandmother (her Indian name before marriage was Nellie Saint John the Baptist) was an Abenaki Indian, from Canada. Her father's name was Iron Knife.

Almost on cue, he pulled his knife. "I bet," he told me with a slight smirk, "that so great a woodsman as you knows how to skin a panther."

"No," I said. "But if you'll allow me to watch, I'm willing to learn. In fact, I'll lend you a hand if I can."

I watched him using the knife. There was little to be gained by more talk. Sometimes, when two men work silently together, more gets done.

He used the knife well. Even though wanting to stand closer, to observe, I kept my distance, more for Charlie than for me. After three days in the swamp, my body and my clothes didn't smell very social. Seminoles inhale well, I imagined. Therefore, it was not my intention to allow Charlie Moon Sky to wrinkle his nose, proving that my clan smelled muckier than his. Earlier, I'd been caught in an Everglades downpour. My khaki shirt, already soiled with sweat, stunk beyond ripe. Without thinking, I moved an inch closer.

"You smell," he told me.

"I do today. Not always. Please remember that I'm a long way from my home in Orlando."

He raised his eyebrows. "Well," he told me, "you said the word *please.* My ears do not hear that often."

"I'll say it again. Because I want to own a knife like yours. Please make me one and I'll pay you a hundred dollars."

He held up his weapon. "For a knife?"

"Yes. A new knife, with no panther blood to disgrace it."

"I will do it," he said. Then his eyes narrowed. "What if I make you a knife but you don't return here to get it?"

Handing him a one-hundred-dollar bill, I said, "In that case, you keep the money and the knife."

He didn't accept the money. Instead, he gave it back to me, and I returned Ben Franklin to his distinguished company.

Looking at me, he said, "You and I become *ocholotatees.*" (I can't spell or speak it right.)

"What's that?"

"Enemies who talk."

"We are not enemies," I said. "Both of us have American Indian blood." (I avoided that insensitive term *Native American.*) "We, in different ways, respect panthers."

Standing close to him, I blessed my British bloodline that helped me to grow to four inches over six foot. Regardless of what you may think, height means leverage. I smiled down at him.

It pleased me when he slyly returned my grin from below, and then told me, "I would have made you a knife for only fifty dollars."

"A bargain is a bargain. I'll pay a hundred. But I expect the best knife that a hunter could ever own."

Over two months passed until I returned to South Florida, to his territory. Because he was a loner, Charlie wasn't easy to locate. Finally did. No, he hadn't yet made me a knife, because his sister had died. It would be improper to prepare a weapon during a period of mourning.

"How long will you mourn?"

To answer, Charlie Moon Sky held up all of his fingers, five times. "Fifty years." Then he relaxed his face muscles and informed me that he had made a joke. We ate together. Gator tail. It tastes like burnt chicken. Without telling me what it was, he served some to me on a roasting stick. Luckily, I recognized it, as some Floridians would.

"You want a knife?"

"Yes."

"Do you still have the one hundred dollars?"

Yanking it out, I showed it to him.

"Good. I make a knife."

During my third visit, the knife became mine to keep. It was crudely handsome, sturdy, and I told him so as I paid him. Its sheath was much longer than the knife itself. He explained why: As a man's hand hangs down from his shoulder, it rests exactly beside the knife's handle. The sheath is secured from above by a belt; from below, by a leg thong, a shoelace-thin lanyard of twisted deer gut, a substance also used to make a bowstring. No knife is properly worn at a man's hip, but rather at the outside of his upper thigh. Here it stays, unless it's being used. At night, Charlie Moon Sky said, the knife sleeps in another scabbard.

His right hand.

Overall, this variation of Seminole knife is about thirteen inches long, including a four-inch handle. The wood is oak, now quite hard, but cut when the wood was green. A sprinkle of tiny colored stones, fragments, are embedded in its handle wood as decoration. Then the entire handle is dipped in warm resin, as a coating. The iron blade is smelted from ore, flattened by a hammer, honed by grinding it on a whetstone. It is crude, yet artistic.

"A knife is like a coral snake," Charlie Moon Sky told me. "Not long, but beautiful and bloody."

He showed me how to draw a knife. Never snatch the handle. Instead, in one graceful motion, a hand merely *wipes* the knife from its sheath. The thumb is forward, pointing downward, and the fingers guide the handle upward until the knife becomes horizontal. A blade is low and raw, ready to strike with its single fang of death.

I had to ask him a question.

"Has your knife ever stabbed a person?"

"No. A man carries a knife not to cause pain, but to prevent it. To protect kindness. All of Nature has weaponry. A pretty flower can be armed with thorns." He smiled. "Besides," he said, "for me, a knife isn't a weapon. It's a tool."

Again and again, I kept pulling my new toy from its sheath, to look at it and to heft its balance in my hand. "Charlie, this is the finest knife I will ever own. Thank you for making it."

"Good." He nodded once. "I am pleased for you. Now it is yours to carry. Be careful. The blade is sharp."

"I'll be cautious. You have my promise that I will not dishonor you by abusing your knife."

"Be sharp enough to own it."

Charlie and I stopped being enemies, yet never became friends. In a sense, we were the last Mohicans, two men representing ancient tribes at war. Too old to continue battle. I confess, I never really liked him. Nor did he take to me. Perhaps we fascinated one another: a mongoose and a cobra.

Knowing him, I once mused, was close to having a citrus rat in your flower bed. It might be folly to get too close, or to trust it. There is a gap between a truce and a trust. I felt Charlie didn't trust me. Why should he? I was never forced to live on a reservation, or railroaded to Oklahoma, or humiliated, or denied my way of life. There was, I always sensed, a quiet fire inside Charlie Moon Sky. Contained yet smoldering, graying to ashes.

Charlie died a number of years ago.

Did he die as he had lived, alone? Knowing his time had come, seeking the endless sea of grass in South Florida, perhaps to climb a cypress so old and so tall that it reaches beyond the sky?

Is there a Nine Man Tree? If so, no living man, young or old, could ever hope to climb it.

Only a soul.

# Warm Quilts

FLORIDA FELT CHILLY THAT MORNING.

I'd stopped for gasoline at an outdated two-pump station beside a red-clay road on the Florida Panhandle.

Research, for my dough, is not library work. It's finding the back paths—lonely, beckoning—and scouting rural areas. Prospecting. There are dirt roads aplenty here, connecting Florida and Georgia and Alabama. A good place to strike gold among grit.

A frayed rope had been strung horizontally from the front corner of the fill-up station to a pine tree that stood seventy feet away. The rope sagged with homespun merchandise. On the pine, a crudely lettered sign read:

## WARM QUILTS

I'd seen close to a dozen signs for QUILTS along these roads and had resisted considering a purchase. This particular sign felt cozy. Warm.

Nearby stood an elderly woman wearing a ratty old Army coat, a gray scarf, no stockings, and a pair of man's shoes. Knowing nothing about shopping for roadside bedding, I walked to the nearest quilt, one in two colors. Yellow and white. The quilt's maker had somehow captured sunshine and woven the strips of cloth into a rectangle of solar strength.

My hand touched its softness.

The old woman approached me. "I call that'n 'Sunday Morning,'" she said, in a voice as gentle and comforting as her quilt. "I give 'em all a name."

Walking along in front of the row of quilts, I stopped at each one, allowing the quilter to introduce us.

"'Benevolence,'" she said, "because there's five different shades of blue, and all of 'em's so kindly."

Her third quilt was neither rectangular nor square. Instead, it was octagonal, featuring what appeared to be eight characters, in pairs. Four maroon, all larger and plainer than the four smaller ones, which were frilly, in pink.

"'Barn Dance,'" she said, silently clapping her hands, "on account it looks like promenade your partner. Years back, when I was a young girl . . . oh, how I could square-dance. And clog. My toes flew like wrens."

"Did *you* make all these quilts?"

She nodded. "Ever single one. You'll see a **HH** down yonder in ever corner. A trademark. My name is Hosannah Holbert."

Touching the brim of my cowboy hat, I bent her a grin. "Nice to meet you, Miss Hosannah. I'm Rob."

"I'll turn seventy-seven come May. Been at quilting for over sixty year." She shook her head. "Young girls today don't do a lick of it. Leastwise not the bubblegummers I meet up."

"What's this next one called?"

It was black and white, with eight durable objects; yet the powerful pattern seemed to be more might than music, so I doubted it represented a dance.

"Them there's oxen," she said. "Holsteins. They's all black-and-white, them cattle, so I named this'n 'Ox Pull.' See? I weave two ox in each of the four corners, facing out. All pullin' like fury. Four yoke. When it's spread out flat to a bed, why, them ox tug so strong you'd swear the quilt was growing and growing."

"It's beautiful work," I said.

"That's because it's usual pleasing to chore at

something you enjoy. Not once—no, not even a one time—did I ever fashion the same quilt twice. Quilts are my children. Each'll git a fresh face. Like a sheet of cookies."

"Makes sense."

"This'n I call 'Attic Window.' If you stand still and study on it, you'll begin to feel you perch away up high, looking out across a meadow of flowers." She leaned an inch or two closer to me. "I hate selling 'em. It pains to part with kin."

"Yes, I suppose it does," I said. "I've often wondered how a painter can stand to sell a painting. He has it one minute, and poof! It's clean gone."

Hosannah looked at the sky.

"At night, after I trade away one of my quilts, I look up to the stars and pretend I can still behold it, spread out across God's bed." Lowering her gaze, she squinted at me for a moment. Then she so slowly smiled. "That's a lot like life itself. Having and losing."

I agreed. "Living is a gain and then a loss."

"What's so sad," Hosannah said, "is that I'll eventual sell all seven of these quilts, and each one'll leave and wander off in a strange direction. To a different place. They'll never again be a family like now, all in line, as though sitting to a supper and blessing their food. Or side by side in a church pew."

Insanity struck me!

"Would you be willing," I asked her, "to allow me to purchase all seven of your quilts? Because I want *all* of them. Right now, before I change my crazy mind."

She blinked a few times.

"All seven?"

"Yes. I'll keep them, give them a good home, and they'll be together. Our family and our guests, snuggled beneath your family."

Hosannah let out a sigh. "That'd be righteous." As she spoke, her smile was warmer than any coverlet.

We sealed the deal.

Happily, I headed for home, wondering how to justify such a spree of impulse buying. As it turned out, no problem. We Pecks are all a tad tilted, so everyone understood. And did so again, a couple of years later, when I collected the quilts, loaded all seven in my car, and drove north to the Panhandle to do research—and to visit Hosannah, of **HH** fame.

She was there. It was a warm homecoming of seven prodigal quilts welcomed by their creator. Eight joyous souls, like a . . .

Barn Dance.

# Movement

THE BAR WAS QUITE DARK.

And very noisy, a blend of yelling and fighting and canned reggae being played louder than a civilized ear can tolerate. Music declaring war.

Being an intruder, I was dressed as the other men were. Poorly. Everyone around me was brown or black, either from Jamaica or Haiti. I had dishonestly charred my face with Florida muck and tied a twisted red bandanna around my head as a headband.

My complexion is naturally dark. Here, it helps.

On this particular night, I was in Belle Glade, Florida, beneath the belly of Lake Okeechobee. It was winter, but warm. The harvesting season for sugarcane. Straddling a barstool, I ordered beer from a bottle, refusing to put a glass or a fork (or even one of the willing young ladies) near my mouth. Most voices spoke English, others French. I can speak both, or so I always thought; except here, where I couldn't clearly understand either.

A cutter on the next barstool fired a joint.

His first drag was hot and deep and demanding, as though his lungs were desperate for disease. Holding the marijuana smoke inside, he held it as long as possible, then exhaled from one nostril. The other must have been clogged. Looking at me, he offered me a free hit.

I grinned, touching a finger to my throat as if to explain why I was refusing his generosity.

"Thank you," I told him. "I can't smoke."

He smiled imperfect teeth. "Hey, that is okay, mon. No problem." After his next inhale he said the obvious. "You not Jamaica."

I shook my head.

"Where?"

"Here, in Florida." Offering an open right hand, I said, "Roberto."

We shook.

"They call me Movement," he said, "or some-time Move." One more pull on the joint. "What you doing in cane-cutter bar?" His eyebrows raised. "Look for young woman, eh?"

"No," I said, much too quickly.

Holding up a finger, he warned, "Hey, don't put no pansy Yankee hands to my body. Mon, I am straight. You dig?"

"I dig. Me too."

"Movement is not my real name."

Tempted to say "Nor am I truthfully Roberto," I held quiet. In bars such as this one, nobody asks for a name, and few offer identification, formal or informal. Fake green cards, a big business, are kept out of sight.

"Why do they call you Movement?"

Wordlessly, he serpentined off the barstool, turned around once, leaped, waved his arms, bent to retrieve a bottle cap from the filthy floor, tossed it up, and caught it. All in one symphonic motion. He wasn't solid. Instead, he was fluid and breeze, flowing and billowing as a ballet. As he whirled, everyone noticed, watching with the same fascination as I did, even though (from those I had observed) many Jamaicans are graceful. To call Movement a dancer would be unjustly inadequate. He wasn't merely a dancer.

He was *dance*.

There was nothing effeminate about him. He appeared to be a total male, so confident of his own swaggering masculinity that he was comfortable with grace. Even his hands were delicate. But not all soft or silken. Movement's handshake had been forcefully firm. Yet a man of lace, a child born of ferns, hemlock, or cypress.

"Move," someone said to him, "do some more."

So he did.

Realizing that all eyes were now focusing on him, Movement gracefully performed, to charm us as easily as a cobra slithering from a wicker basket. As he danced, the reggae began to make sense, because Movement added meaning. He swayed to each note as though creating it on a sheet of music with his body as a feathery quill. He was a perfect visual interpretation of sound.

For a moment, a young black girl danced with Movement as his partner. Yet, despite that she was lithe and pretty, I found myself watching him instead of her. When he danced, or walked, or shifted to another position on a barstool, all eyes followed Movement, mine included.

"Mon," he laughed, "I got style."

In sequence, half a dozen girls danced with Movement, each reluctantly releasing him to the next partner. He coaxed them to improve, to leap, to fly.

People bought and brought Movement drinks, one after another. He thanked everyone, his black eyes flashing as though he deserved the attention in which he was basking. To every lady, he bowed. When he did so, even an adolescent bar harlot imagined, perhaps, that she had become a princess, a king's daughter, or the beloved sweetheart of a prince. Movement drank. He smoked, danced, shouted to me within an inch of my ear because the music was as loud as the crowd.

"Where," I asked Movement, "did you learn to dance the way you do? You really are good, you know. More than good. You're the best dancer I've ever seen."

"Want to know who teach me?"

"Yes, I do."

"No problem." He giggled boyishly. "Fred Astaire."

I laughed too, prompted by the fact that Fred Astaire had retired before this lad was born.

"Old movies," Movement told me. "In Jamaica, only rich go to new movies. Us peoples see old gray mares. That where I meet Mr. Fred Astaire."

The evening got later, and drunker, and I would have offered a sawbuck for a lungful of fresh air. Yet as long as Movement danced, or even paraded to the men's room, I had to tarry and watch his return.

Next morning, however, came very early.

It was Wednesday.

On Tuesday, the day before, I'd taken careful notice where the burners were burning the fields of sugarcane. Growers burn on the day before they harvest. No sugar company wants an author (or a reporter) to visit a cutter camp or a cane field. I was officially told that no cane chopper permitted himself to be photographed.

Cameras, in Clewiston and Moore Haven and LaBelle, were regarded with mistrust. To be photoed was bad luck. A camera was merely one more white man's demon.

A devil box.

For a few bucks, Movement smuggled me into the camp. His temporary domicile, loosely described, was an unpainted cement-block structure of one story, one room, with neither stove nor electricity, and no working toilet. Disguised as I was, I slept unnoticed with about a dozen other men in a room that stunk of sweat and filth and hopelessness.

To a cane cutter, such is home.

I had my own cane knife.

Carrying it, I boarded a dull-green school bus the next morning, before dawn. The darkness protected me from detection, masking my identity, allowing me to chop sugarcane (at almost the age of sixty) with men who were one-third my age.

Movement was my sponsor.

First off, he called me Tall, or Tall Guy, a moniker that suited me because I am, after all, a tall guy. Cane, I learned, is not chopped from an erect position. We cutters are only erect from the waist down. The upper body remains horizontal.

The first hour isn't bad.

Beneath me, the smoking land was blackened, charred by Tuesday's burn. Every twenty yards, I'd discover a dead animal . . . rat, possum, rabbit, even a dog. A young pig! It had been trapped and roasted alive.

I didn't eat the pork. The Jamaicans, however, tore it apart, and it disappeared in minutes.

Foolishly, I had brought nothing to drink. As the day heated, my throat was parched with smoke dust coupled with backbreaking work. Movement unscrewed his jug of "petrol" and gave me its virgin swig. The name has no connection with gasoline or any other petroleum product. It is merely a field beverage, brought along in plastic-gallon milk containers . . . a blend of dark beer, tomato juice or V8, spices (usually cinnamon or nutmeg), and eggnog, plus a can of condensed milk.

It was poison, but I was parched.

"Petrol," said Movement, "give a mon power for work, and then be stamina for love."

The local young black ladies adore Jamaican men, Movement bragged, claiming that they are handsome and more generous (because they work harder and longer, and get paid more), and because Jamaicans are lean and muscular. Add to all this their enchanting accent. They sing instead of talk.

Movement danced through the day.

With grace, ease, and never an awkward motion or a false step, his cane knife arched its silvery half-circle, cutting and slashing, as if the two of them, and their activity, had been choreographed by some Broadway director.

Nonetheless, it was still hard labor. American blacks refuse to do it. Cane chopping is not artistry. It's a means of survival for Jamaicans and Haitians. And me. Not because I needed to cut sugarcane to exist. I had to do it to learn enough to write not a book, but at least an accurate chapter.

A fight started.

Some cutter trespassed on another man's petrol and the silver blades of cane knives were crimson with hot blood. Men shouted. Swore. Bosses came in Jeeps and Rovers, guns fired, and a dog barked.

Jamaicans fear a dog. And any snake.

"If you knife-cut a snake, mon," Movement informed me seriously, "the poison fly up, and it blind you bad. Forever. And it blind you children back home in the islands."

It would be immoral, I concluded, to tell Movement that his beliefs were false. Rightfully, one can't rob a man of his inherent philosophy unless able to instantly replace it with a wiser one. Who could say which tenets were correct? Those of a

Jamaican cane chopper or of a Vermont farm boy turned author?

It was the longest day of my entire semi-retired life, but somehow I made it to sundown.

A bus, this one blue, returned us to the cutter camp. A very large Hispanic crew boss locked the gate behind us. Never presume that field hands, regardless of color or nationality, live a great deal more freely than prior to Emancipation.

After work, we sat shirtless, unable to stir or eat or sleep or breathe, or prepare a meal. Pain pounded my spine. I was too exhausted to unwrap from my wrists and ankles the protective bandages that Movement had provided for my safety. Everywhere, eyes were staring at other faces. Somewhere, a cutter was sharpening his cane knife, rasping a file to and fro across the edge of a metal blade. I could smell cookery of some sort, possible red beans and rice, collards, and a mash of supermarket junk that the local merchants sold to all the cutters at a boosted price.

The whores came.

Each woman brought a blanket and a bottle or two of cheap wine. Movement bought himself a jump. He invited me to tag along in order to observe his prowess. Politely, I declined. Listening to the bickering that eventually determined her price was enough of an education. The prostitutes were all ages. None tempting. Already I had contracted herds of body lice, which were now galloping through the tundra of my southern hemisphere like a panic of lemmings.

In the night, I began to ponder if the people at the Clewiston Inn were wondering of my whereabouts. I was truly wondering myself.

At havens of Okeechobee respectability, such as the Clewiston Inn or the Port LaBelle Inn, I am known as Mr. Peck, a successful author. There, no one calls me Tall Guy or asks me to douse my thirst with a sip from a plastic milk-jug of petrol.

At hotels, no one scratches.

At sugarcane camps, everyone does.

For me, it was a challenge to gain entrance into a labor camp. Now, lying in the dark, afraid, awaiting Movement's return from his metered romancing, I began to wonder if I could escape from this sewer and return to soap, and sanity. Nearby, there was a toilet bowl. A stagnant puddle of brown smelly filth. No toilet paper. A gray core was hanging uselessly from a triangular wire.

Movement returned.

I expected him to be smiling.

He wasn't. Instead, he seemed depressed, as if he had sold himself into a lower level of society and fouled his body. Also his wife.

"Tall Guy!" he hollered above the constant

noise of fighting, gambling, and a poorly function-
ing radio on batteries. "Mon, I hope I don't catch a
misery. Had it a one time. Hurt like a whip to pee."

He lay quiet.

Near us, two cutters were playing dominoes,
banging each little black brick on a plywood square
supported by cement blocks, yelling and trying to
shave the odds. Each domino was played with such
untamed force, as though the players had decided
that noise and violence tallied up a win.

Before dawn, I hid and escaped, clawing earth
and crawling under a chain fence, through buggy
water, to freedom. A schoolteacher stopped his
Toyota to offer me a lift. A do-gooder not yet
mugged. I was, however, oh so grateful. He never
told me his name. I retained mine. We rode by
another camp, littered with wastepaper and beer
cans and empty wine bottles.

"May I drop you in town?"

I surprised him with ten dollars. "No, thank
you. Please cart me as close to the Clewiston Inn as
you dare. I'm much too dirty and exhausted to
explain in any relevant Aristotelian logic."

His mouth fell a foot.

I ducked in the back door of the Clewiston Inn,
on the north side, and sneaked by the cocktail
lounge, which is on the right as one enters. My hall
ran to the left.

Following a bath, a shave, and a generous application of paratox (a product used to rid one of head lice, body lice, crab lice, and their countless eggs), I stretched out on a clean and unslept-on bed, hoping that the liquid parasiticide was exterminating my little guests and their progeny. The next day I also tried dog shampoo. It all worked.

I kept thinking of Movement.

One evening more than a month later, I returned to the cutter camp, bribing a gate guard with a twenty and a jug of wine. It took a while to find the cement-block structure where I'd slept. Where he'd slept. Men were inside, cooking, arguing, punching each other, laughing, gambling at dominoes and Blackjack and Casino. They were drinking the cheap wine that a cutter was forced to buy, thirsty or not.

"You seen Movement?" I asked a cutter, then another, and more.

Nobody said a word. No man would admit that he had ever known Move or watched him dance. Movement had simply disappeared, evaporated as milk into the unknown plastic container that is a Sugarland harvest of lives as well as cane.

"Is he dead?"

No answer.

I can only conclude that he is. A cane knife across a throat can snuff a man very quickly. And everywhere in the Okeechobee area run canals and ditches, a thousand nooks to stash a corpse. You could hide a horse.

Possibly there's a chance that certain sugarcane choppers go to Heaven, a clean place where there are no long sun-scorching days, no green buses. But there has to be music. Because somewhere a talented Jamaican is dancing and gliding gracefully to some celestial reggae.

Even if there's no music at all, angels will certainly hear it as soon as they see Movement dance.

# The Jeeters

I HAD TO STOP MY TRUCK.

Pulling off the red-clay road, I jumped down from the cab of my pickup and walked back about thirty or forty feet.

"You deserve saving."

Picking up the large dark-green turtle, I was surprised how heavy it felt. A big one, dishpan size. Its shell could have served as Goliath's war helmet. Carrying it to the road's edge, I hopped a ditch, fixing to release the turtle to a cactus patch, in shade. Beyond the cactus was a stand of low-growing palmetto that the Florida swampers call fan palms. Two main varieties. Smooth-stalked and thorny. This was thorny: little curly barbs (on a brown stem) that can chew at flesh and near eat it.

Setting the turtle down and straightening up, I

made that alarming one-second discovery that I wasn't alone. Between a pair of palmetto shrubs, there was a human face, staring at me.

Not for long.

Eyes now looked at the turtle. From a distance of ten yards, I could identify a child's face. Very lean, and very dirty. Long stringy hair that appeared not to have known a comb or a brush. A little girl. Moving a step or two to my right, I saw more of her. Her shabby dress seemed to have no color. Just cloudy. She pointed at the turtle. I guessed that she might have been after it as I'd stopped the truck and that she was concerned I was going to rob the turtle for myself.

"Hello," I said.

No reply. As expressionless eyes continued to study me, she neither advanced nor fled. Her age was perhaps eight or nine. Thin arms. Circling her unwashed mouth was a black ring of grease.

"My name's Rob."

No response.

Until now, the turtle had been as motionless as the little girl. Then a head appeared, a tail, four clawed feet. He crawled forward, unhurried as turtles are. Not interested in the turtle but curious about this child, I followed.

"Where are you going?" I asked him. His flat cream-colored belly shell was drawing a smooth trail on the loose sand, with a double border of claw swipes. The turtle track reminded me of marks left by an Army tank.

I followed the turtle.

The little girl followed me.

Of the three of us, I was the only one who contributed to the conversation, but no sophisticate could label it inspired chatter.

"Better hurry," I advised the turtle. "Because this young lady and I are after you and it'll be a cinch to catch up."

We all stopped. I stopped because the turtle did. She stopped, I presumed, because I had. Then a guess. Pointing at the turtle, and to her, I made signs that suggested she wanted the turtle for food. If not a turtle, she certain was in need of some other dish, because this child was close to bone-skinny. Too close.

"Are you hungry?"

She nodded.

"Me too," I said. "What's your name?" No answer. "My name's Robert, or Rob, mostly." I thought for a moment or two. "Maybe you and I ought to capture that big ol' turtle and eat him for supper."

She shook her head. Then, to my amazement, spoke.

"I fetch him to home."

Florida, 1977. Turtle and Dove, pony mare and foal, a filly.

Smiling, I nodded, and told her, "Okay, he's all yours. Not mine. Because you probable saw him first." To substantiate my intent, I pointed to myself and shook my head. Then, pointing to the turtle and to her, I nodded.

Running to the turtle, she tried to lift it, but couldn't. Oh, perhaps a couple of inches, but that was about it. Setting the turtle down, she looked at me helplessly, as though fixing to sob or run away.

I went to her.

"Please don't cry," I said. Bending, I picked up the turtle, realizing why such a burden was too much for her to tote. "Which way, and how far?"

Saying nothing, she walked away briskly, looking over a bony shoulder to check if I followed. Again, as I walked, I noticed her dress. A pathetic rag. Suitable, however, for Florida heat, perhaps only in the privacy of a swamp. Earlier, I'd seen no indication that the little girl wore any underwear. Needless to add, she was barefoot, including dirty legs, ankles, and toes. But kids have a right to get dirty.

The turtle was becoming heavier.

I was starting to realize that this whopper was the largest turtle I'd ever lifted. Or carried. Believe this for sure, his tail was to my belt buckle, head forward. At the moment, he was totally withdrawn from society, and I was grateful for his momentary hermitage.

"Brother," I told my turtle friend, "give up desserts."

As I glanced at the trusting little girl, now walking ten steps in front of me, it seemed plausible that this child had never eaten even one dessert in her lifetime.

Moving further and further inland, I was wondering if I'd again locate my truck. The landscape changed. Closer to the road, the trees that we had passed beneath had been pines and oaks, a few sycamores in full leafy green. Behind me the earth had been firm, harder and dryer. Here, however, the dirt was a soft, blacker muck.

More ferns.

Along the road, high ground, I'd heard the musical variety of mockingbirds and the sharp *chit chit chit* of cardinals. No longer. As I walked along, I noticed more wading birds, long-legged white cranes and blue herons. Frogs and cicadas seemed to be tuning up, stilling as we passed, then resuming their constant choir. I saw a white ibis standing silently on one long slender leg, her scimitar beak cocked and ready to become a weapon.

On my right was a dead bell-bottom cypress.

My nose sensed muscadine and wild coffee. All the smells were damper now, cooler and more intense. A Florida swamp, if you're unfamiliar with it, has a way of suddenly surrounding you, with no north, south, east, or west. Just a jungle of green.

Large leaves hang thicker, lower, more entangling.

Ahead of me, the child was walking a definite path, serpentining around black puddles of swamp water, ducking in between the long, dangling vines, some of which were stouter than wharf rope. A wood duck, displaying his rainbow of plumage, darted across a small pond of dark water, his V-shaped wake spreading to both banks.

I breathed moist greenish air.

But smelled smoke.

As the little girl stopped, she turned and pointed at a log shack, on stilts because of the wet terrain. A wispy scar of gray smoke was scraping its lazy line upward into the high greeny lace of cypress. Reaching her home at last, I put the turtle down, almost dropping him from my tiring arms.

A thin woman appeared at the door.

Her dress was identical to the little girl's. The same cloudy cottony material, no pattern or color, only larger. My guess was that this woman had possible sewed both garments. Her hand clutched a can of beer.

"Hello," I said. "We brought you a turtle."

A dog came, quickly arched its back, and growled. From all I could see, it was a black-and-tan coonhound. The dog looked as poor as the people. The woman's hair was long and yellowy white, totally unstyled, hanging in witch's tangles front and back. Her skin was old, grayer than aging concrete.

"Who you be?" she asked, burping.

"I'm Robert."

Briefly she looked at the motionless meal, then at the child (too young to be a daughter), and back to me.

"Who?"

"Robert. Rob Peck. If you demand to know my full name, it's Robert Newton Peck." I grinned. "But

I don't know the little girl's name, or yours."

If I expected an answer, I didn't get one. Only stares from two aging eyes that appeared to be neither alive nor dead.

"Jeeter," the child told me.

A name isolated, especially if it's unfamiliar, rarely sounds like a name. Merely like a noise. A bird call. Here, from all sides, I could hear birds, bugs, frogs—a steady throbbing swamp song of endless tempo. An eerie backdrop to one more natural chirp.

"Jeeter," the girl said again. "We's be Jeeters. Like you. All peoples got Jeeter for a name."

Her little voice was as soft as her dress. A sound of cotton. Almost no sound at all. Uneducated, unspoiled, she spoke so slowly.

I asked a dumb question. "Do you go to school?"

Her sustained silence, however, was providing answer enough. She didn't know what *school* meant. It would be silly, and rude, to explain to these two people that I was an author. For once, I resisted trying to impress the ladies. Appraising the coon dog, I decided not to move around too much, or too quickly. The dog's teeth were bared. The black hair along the dog's spine had bristled erect, the shoulder bones up, as if it was concentrating on a larger-than-customary human.

I turned away, to the little girl.

"So, your name is Jeeter. What's your other name?"

"Belly."

"Your name is Belly Jeeter."

"Belle. My granny say Belly sometime."

"Oh, I see."

Without another word, Granny Jeeter took her beer and disappeared back inside the shack. The dog stayed. Belle started picking up pieces of dry wood. Seeing what she was doing, I helped her.

"Belle . . . Belle?"

She looked my way, holding a stick.

"Do you have a mama, or a daddy?"

Scowling, she said, "I got me Granny," sounding as though she was surprised I didn't thoroughly understand.

"Just the two of you?"

"Three. We's got a dog. He be a Jeeter dog."

"Yes, of course."

Dropping the wood she had been carrying, Belle scratched her head, curving the delicate fingers of her right hand into an inflexible claw, digging at her scalp. Head lice, one could presume. If I could ever find this place again (better yet, and more importantly, first find my way *out*), I'd bring Belle a bottle of dog shampoo. Industrial-strength.

All around this shack, the ground was littered

with debris, leftovers of junk food, bread wrap, empty cigarette packs, a plastic six-ring holder from a six-pack beverage of unknown brand. And there were countless empty cans everywhere. Beer. Beer. Beer.

Litter is a fact of life, I suppose.

Where the Jeeters resided was a spot of natural savage beauty. Except for ugly humanity. I smiled. Here I stood, the largest hunk of humanity in sight; ergo, the biggest litter problem. At least the Jeeters would *eat* a turtle. How many times had my powerful, expensive cars hit and killed a road animal, leaving it behind, unused?

Together we built a fire in an outdoor pit. Using a bucket and making several trips, I filled the pot with swamp water. Once it was angrily boiling, the giant turtle's life ended in a second or two. We cooked it, shell and all.

I ate very little.

Not because I dislike turtle meat, but because I was observing how skinny little Belle and lean old Granny tore at their portions. Hands stinging from the hot meat, they couldn't wait for it to cool. Turtle flesh is an acquired taste, one I never fully acquired. A turtle, like a turkey, has several different varieties of meat, all edible if your dietary standards are adequately relaxed.

"This is good," I lied.

Belle and Granny just chewed.

With a rock, I busted apart the complete shell so the coonhound could munch too. He did, cracking a few bones with his teeth, tail wagging. Years ago, in a swamp one night, camping with a Calusa friend, I happened to hear a similar noise, very loud. A cracking, crunching report.

"What was that?" I'd asked.

"Gator."

"Killing something?"

The Calusa nodded. "Big turtle."

This is the Florida that is real, the one that tourists never see, or hear, or taste.

It is forest, swamp, and untamed survival. Best of all, it is sharing a fresh-boiled turtle with a very old swamper and a very young one.

Granny and Belle.

A year later (believe it or not, with a bag of oranges, bread, a white plastic bottle of shampoo, and a comb), I tried to find my way back to visit the Jeeters. After a few futile starts, I located the place. The shack was gone, destroyed, and little of it remained. Some of the local litter had begun to decay. With a sigh, I policed the area, tidying up as neatly as I could, burying the trash.

"Belle," I called a few times, hoping.

Only the frogs answered.

# Best Friend

VALOR.

This is the name my dog answers.

Years ago, I had only to whisper his name and he'd come. Now he is almost deaf, so as a courtesy I go to him. Sensing me, knowing my smell, a broken tail thumps the floor in welcome. Then slowly, with groanings of painful age, he forces himself to rise, ready for duty.

Valor is thinner now, almost fragile, no longer the burly coon hunter and bear tracker. I cannot ask him to splash into cold water to retrieve a fallen canvasback. Or drive a deer to my watch.

Frequently he naps indoors, seeking patches of sunlight to ease his stiffness. His eyes, which once shined brighter than horse chestnuts, are now cloudy, a look of winter. I must be careful not to rearrange furniture, for if I do, Valor may bump an uncustomary chair, and then appear to be shamed by his clumsiness.

As a hunter, his bark once sounded with orchestral variety, announcing a rabbit, a fox, a treed coon . . . or that he had found water or my truck.

Valor's body has been bitten by a rattlesnake, raked by panther claws, hit by a car, kicked by a horse as well as by his former owner. Yet pain never soured his rapture for life. Except once, and then only briefly. Valor came whimpering home one night, his soft muzzle bristling with porcupine quills. Head in my lap, he lay trembling as my pliers removed each bloody spear.

He trusted me to do this unpleasant task, somehow knowing it had to be done, licking gratitude upon my face when I told him the last quill had been extracted.

Valor is deaf, blind, lame.

Today I must take a shovel and a pistol. The two of us will stroll our final outing together. A grave will be dug somewhere in woods where he used to hunt, or merely race the wind. Somehow he will know that what I'm about to do for him is just and merciful. One of my many quirks that he accepts.

No veterinarian's needle will terminate his

life in foreign environs. He will not die among strangers. Valor's end must be private and dignified. For my dog, I promise that his death shall be painless.

Only his friend will feel the pain.

# Spook and Rita

I MET THEM IN A DINER.

One of those pewtery Florida cow-town diners with a plain name that you're as eager to forget as its decor. Not much of a seating choice. No table. Pick a narrow booth or a hard stool. As every booth was occupied, I took the counter.

Back in the kitchen, a radio was wailing a sad cowboy song. Merle was sounding more sorrowful than a flat puddle of flat beer.

A plump waitress, perhaps beyond her prime (me too), eyed me as I wishboned my legs to fork the stool's torn leatherette top. Her uniform, half a size too small, was a skimpy white waitress dress trimmed with pink piping. A plastic Mickey Mouse head pinned a cheap lace handkerchief, folded fluffy to resemble a corsage, just north of an ample breast.

Beneath her opposite shoulder, a slightly warped name tag announced something about her life as well as her name: RITA.

"Coffee?" she asked.

"Please. Hot and black, Rita."

"You got it, cowboy."

After filling a white mug, Rita pivoted on the Cuban heel of a white Red Cross, landed the sloshing mug on the smeared counter in front of me, cracked her gum, and raised one eyebrow with what I guessed was a rehearsed gesture.

"Need a menu?"

"Thanks."

Without reading it, I could probable predict what the breakfast menu was fixing to offer.

"Good Morning!" was its opening salvo at the top of the single see-through yellowing card. It was morning for sure. Early. On the clock over the coffeemaker, both black hands hanged into five thirty-three like a Fu Manchu mustache. Eyeing the menu instead of Rita's generosity, I considered: one egg, two eggs, three eggs, ham, bacon, sowbelly, biscuits and gravy, golden pancakes (large or small stack), waffles, bass, or catfish. Fried potatoes and grits served gratis with every plate.

Rita returned.

"What'llyagonnahave?" she asked, without her Doublemint breaking stride.

I smiled. Even though Rita had been booked right out of Central Casting, she was perfect, and entertaining. "Eggs," I said with a grin.

"What flavor?"

"Two over medium. And please ask the cook to puncture the yolks so they don't stare at me like I'm babe-naked."

Checking me up and down in less than a second, Rita nodded. "Anything else ya might like, cowboy?"

I cuffed back my beat-up silbelly Stetson. "Two strips of bacon. Crisp. Dry, not slippery. And a hot biscuit. No butter. Just orange marmalade. I'd like my breakfast on a warm plate. And please, when you get a chance, how about a refill on coffee?"

"In a shake." Rita shook herself away. "Nobody can hustle everything to once. I only got one pair."

I'd noticed.

While waiting for my breakfast to burn, or spill, I sipped coffee. It was near strong enough to poison rats, kill weeds, and peel varnish. This was genuine redneck coffee in which you could float a horseshoe. Instead of a taste, it was more like a burn. Or a cut.

Behind me, the screen door squeaked open, paused, then banged shut. An aging cowpoke grunted as he occupied the next stool. His worn knuckles appeared to have been busted in several joints, or in several saloons.

Rita hurried to greet him.

"Hiya, sugar bun," the old man said.

Her smile was genuine, and warmer than a hug in a honeymoon hotel. "Hey, Daddy." Eyes shining, Rita touched his leathery hand, giving it a quick pat. She handed him a rumpled paper. "Here's the news, darlin'. So read up."

Her father took it and squinted at the headlines, pulling his head back enough to fake reading.

*"You,"* Rita scolded, "didn't git your eyeglasses fixed. I told you I'd spring for 'em." Reaching across the counter, she tested the one breast pocket on his gray work shirt. "And they're to *home* . . . where they won't do you no good at all."

"But it cost twenty dollars," he said.

"Well," she said, "I ain't got a half of it. But maybe by the end of the morning, when Thelma comes, I'll have twenty. If we git a booth crowd of butt pinchers."

Nodding like a chastised child, he quickly changed the subject.

"I got me a job, Rita."

"Where at?"

"Over to the rodeo arena."

"Doing *what*?" she asked, fists on her hips as though preparing a quick disapproval.

Nova Scotia, 1960. Maris and Mantle. Rodeo stock. Each bull weighed over a ton. Rob at a delicate 230. (Photo by D.A.H.)

"Working one of the chute gates."

My breakfast arrived, by Rita. The plate wasn't hot, yet it wasn't cold either. No complaints. For garnish, there was a slice of orange and a parsley sprig.

"Daddy, I'm fixing to fret at you again. A hundred times you been told how I worry about you and *rodeo work*. Not at your age. I'm trying to keep you safe and me sane."

He sighed. "It's what I know, honey. Since we give up our cattle, working a rodeo's all I can do. I don't handle nothing else."

"Nuts to that," she said. "You could locate a part-time over at Ferguson's Nursery. A geranium don't weigh no three thousand pounds, and it won't kick your guts apart."

Rita flounced off to sling plates at other customers. She really did hustle at her job.

Her daddy turned to me. "She's my daughter. Only child I got. Jacky got kilt about ten year ago. Maybe more. He was my boy. But he bought it bull riding. Skull crushed. Leastwise he didn't die digging up a daisy." As I was nudging eggs across a yellow-stained plate, mopping my mess with half a biscuit that weighed more than a hockey puck, Rita's father introduced himself. "My name is Spellman Gatling."

"Rob Peck."

"People don't usual call me Spellman. I git called Spook mostly, or sometimes Spooker."

"Pleased to know you, Mr. Gatling."

He smiled with sorry teeth. "Golly be, don't nobody much at all ever give me a Mr. Gatling."

"I will, if it's okay."

"Okay." He paused, for some reason. "Rita's my daughter," he said once again, perhaps because of pride, or maybe just plain age. He leaned close. "I eat here for free."

"You're lucky," I lied.

"Yeah," he agreed. "I certain hit it lucky to beget a gal like my Rita Louise. She's awful good. Oh, she'll snap at me. But Rita's a comfort in lots of ways."

"Even if she nags you about glasses?"

Spook muttered something. "Yeah, I s'pose."

"Tell me about your rodeo."

Eyeing my snowy hair, he asked, *"You entering?"*

"No. I'm not young enough to risk my neck. Years ago I tried it once, and it was a pile of pain. A bronc named Undertaker's Pal stuffed everything I owned up into my hat."

Spook Gatling winced. "Bronc riders usual walk strange. Most of 'em are outside bones more broke than the Ten Commandments."

Mr. Gatling made me smile.

He smiled back, which wasn't too easy, seeing as he was understocked in teeth. "I rid bulls," he said. "Didn't stick to the buzzer anytime except once. But it failed to put me into the money."

After braving another gulp of diner coffee, I asked, "Is it hard to earn a living on the rodeo circuit?"

The old man chuckled.

"Naw, it ain't hard. Just impossible."

I laughed too.

"Over at the Silver Spur—that's the rodeo we got going twice a year nearby—you'll spot a plenty old rodeo pokes, like me," Mr. Gatling explained. "They's all chasing poverty on a lame leg. A man don't break a horse as easy as a horse can break a man. Neck or wallet."

Rita arrived with his breakfast.

To me, she said, "Daddy eats the same ho-hummer every morning, day in and day out. Ain't he a *mess*?"

His plate was heaped with white steaming grits, fried spuds, a couple of crumbled biscuits topped with gravy, a few sections of a fresh orange, plus a side order of soft buttered toast. All of it appearing simple to chew. Knuckles up, Mr. Gatling worked a fork with one twisted tine. "Yup, some breakfast. Stick with a winner, my friend, and it'll stick to you. Ribs and spirit."

Spook whacked into his food as if suspecting it was still alive and fixing to escape. I was already outside my breakfast. Although not quite ready to slide off a stool just yet, because I wanted to get to know Spook Gatling. To know Rita Louise as well, but not in a romantic way. Honest.

Gumming grits, Spook looked at me.

"Rita ain't fooling me none," he said.

"Oh, she isn't? How so?"

"She claims that I can take my meals here for nothing. That's not true. Rita pays Henry, her boss, out her own pocket. I mean, whatever I eat is took out of her pay." He sighed. "It bothers more'n I let on. Gnaws at me. Inside. Ought to be *me* helping Rita."

"Is she married with a family?"

"Used to. Billy run off. Left her with a baby, and bills. Never seen Billy again. He was in rodeo too. But quite a time ago, a Saturday night it was, Billy'd tipped up too much booze. He won money that day. So some hot little buckle bunny nabbed him, and they run off together the next afternoon."

"What's a buckle bunny?" I asked, knowing the term, yet hankering to hear Spook's assessment.

"Oh, just a shapely little gal in too-tight jeans that chases one silver-buckle rodeo star after another. A saddle tramp. Anyhow, that's the last Rita Lou and the baby smelt of her husband."

"How old is her baby now?"

"Rita told me recent." He dunked half a slice of toast into his coffee, ate it, and suffered a brown riverlet to drip off his chin to his shirt. "I recall. She's nineteen."

It surprised me.

"Her name's Lark."

"That's a pretty name for a girl."

Rita slapped my check on the counter, face-down. "Come back and see us now. Hear?"

"I'll do it."

When she'd hurried off, Mr. Gatling whispered to me. "Lark ain't normal."

"What's wrong with her?"

"She just never growed up much. And couldn't learn to speak. Makes a few noises, like if'n she's scared, or hungry. Lark don't say things to make sense. It hurts plenty to hear her try. I know it cuts Rita."

I paid my bill at the CASHIER sign at a far end of the counter, near the kitchen door, no doubt positioned where Henry could oversee the transactions. Rita was a cashier as well as a waitress.

"Thank you, Rita."

"You're more'n welcome, cowboy."

"The breakfast was right passable. And delightfully served. You can tell Henry, if you like."

Rita made a face. "I tell that rascal plenty. Mr. Quick Henry and his busy back-room hands."

Her father stood beside me, selecting a toothpick, causing me to wonder how he would employ it.

"It was a pleasure meeting your daddy, Rita," I said. "He's a decent gentleman."

Instead of looking at me, the waitress eyed her father. "No, he ain't. He's a ratty old rodeo-broke scorpion, Spook is. And it's a waste of affection to tolerate him."

"I bet you waste plenty his way."

She winked. "Too dang much."

"Come on," Mr. Gatling said, nudging me. "You and me ought to sneak-stroll over to the arena place and see what's happening. Maybe hoot up some mischief. Or flirt a gal."

His voice sounded eager, as though a rodeo was racing his blood. Spook was itching to play a small, inconsequential role in one more show, and hear another banjo band blasting out "Dixie" or a Rebel yell as a chute gate opened. And stand an inch taller, watching a solitary horse and rider circle the dirt arena at a gallop, flapping Old Glory on a pole.

"A good idea," I said.

"Before noon, Daddy," said Rita, "you best pop around at the eyeglass place, to git your new cheaters. You promised me. Somehow I'll pay 'em their twenty smackers."

He nodded. "Thanks, sugar bun. I'll tend to Lark anytime you need. I looked in earlier. She's asleep. And the dog's on duty."

As she eyed her father and me, Rita's face softened to a gentle smile. "Okay, you two handsome ol' cowbucks go whoop it up. But please try to maintain safe. Hear?"

There was a sign on the cash register: NO NEED TO TIP AT COUNTER. It's always sport to bend a rule. Especially if the so-called tenet doesn't hold a lick of horse sense.

I left a tip for Rita.

For all of Rodeo Week, the happiest twenty bucks I'd fritter away.

# Just as I Am

THE ABOVE HEADING IS ALSO A HYMN.

Haven Peck, the dear father I knew for only the first thirteen years of my life, used to sing it while swinging a scythe to harvest hay on our farm. Or broadcasting seed from a shoulder sack. And, like a hymn, this final chapter is a cleansing by confession, a private peek into my mind.

*Warning:* A simple man might oversimplify. Yet this man prefers point-blank simplicity to complication. The following conclusions are mine only, not intended to be yours by contagion. In fact, I'll be happy if you disagree. Even happier if you ignore my guide irons and forge a few of your own.

1. Movies are funniest when cop cars crash.

2. Our planet Earth is female. Seed her and she'll bear fruit. Our atmosphere (pollen in the wind) is male.

3. People who sweat and have calluses on their hands sound more horse-sensible to me than men with manicures. If I possess wisdom, much of it originated from a father, a mother, an aging aunt, and my American Indian grandmother . . . none of whom could skillfully read or write. An old Vermonter with whom I slaughtered hogs advised me: "Son, work the job you hold with all your might, and you'll not have to work it forever."

4. Strong folks are seldom *offended*. We're too busy accomplishing, helping others, and rapturing in our success.

5. No matter how tender you care about people, you'll not alter anyone. Best afford them the noblest gift a man can offer a neighbor. Acceptance.

6. For fifty years, my dearest pal was probably Fred Rogers, the soft-spoken Mister Rogers of television. He was best man at my wedding. But I could never convince him that his next book should be entitled *Strangers Have the Best Candy*. We were the antithesis of each other, yet disagreed without becoming disagreeable.

7. Maturity has at last enabled my refusing: a flirtatious lady, a shot of Chivas, and a game of poker. But when encountering a piano, I'm irresistibly compelled to play it.

8. A man can be a confirmed atheist and still feel uplifted by the teachings and parables of

one magnificent Nazarene carpenter.

9. My first wife and I were married for thirty-five years. Although divorced, Dorrie and I still are devotedly respectful of one another. We and our current spouses are close friends. Both ladies were librarians.

10. In athletics, if given a choice, I'd prefer to play well and lose, rather than play poorly and win.

11. Book writing is borrowing hunks of leather from leathery folk, tooling them into a saddle, and then riding a wild mustang to meet a bear.

12. Because we destroy the habitats and lives of so many mammals, reptiles, birds, fish, insects, and trees, one might conclude that all of life on Earth is sacred, with the exception of humanity.

13. Health is a personal responsibility. It is not a governmental concern (or a taxpayer's burden) that some people prefer forks to exercise, smoke to fresh air, or booze over orange juice.

14. Women, be wary of men who don't own land. Manhood, like trees, is rooted in earth.

15. The media term *adult language* is a lie. We are telling children that *filth* is grown-up. Years ago, and using a broken Crayola, I was misspelling four-letter *adult language* over a urinal when I was nine.

16. A hero is a gentleman. Among men, reserved gentility takes more guts than home runs or touchdowns.

17. Events I choose to write about are often the tender touchings by rough rogues. Folks I treasure most are the stalwart men and women with whom I performed arduous *labor*. My memory washes their feet. For me, gritty work is more sacred than poetry or prayer.

18. Every honorable Southerner should, with pride, display our Confederate Battle Flag. If we are too spineless to do this, the banner of our heritage will be disgraced in the hands of neo-Nazis, skinheads, members of the Klan, and other loutish lunatics. Considering the fine young men who fought and died for it (a majority were not slave owners), the Stars and Bars deserves to fly upon a loftier staff, in our hearts and in history.

19. Please, just once, let's build a school where the cafeteria is smaller than the library. Better yet, no cafeteria at all. And no junk food or soft drink machines.

20. Schools, once again, ought to be *small* neighborhood schools, and completely autonomous. No systems. And no political busing: kids can walk, strengthen their bodies, and help a taxpayer. Today's huge school invites discipline problems; ergo, who then becomes the principal? A football coach with the I.Q. of a Tic Tac.

21. Communism is a *flop*. It has pathetically failed all over the world.

22. Happiness is being married to my Sam, a brilliant and beautiful Southern lady, granddaughter of Robert E. Lee Youngblood and the finest catfish cook in Dixie. Best of all, she calls me Sweet P.

23. I exalt Dr. Jack Kevorkian far more than doctors who keep elderly patients alive, suffering and paying doctor bills.

24. I won't respect Third World men until they honor Third World women.

25. Research is outdoor work. Getting off pavement and getting dirty.

26. How do you determine if a dog is male or female? Easy. When it drinks from a toilet and leaves the seat up, it's a male.

27. Heaven is a Pearly Gated community.

28. It's always darkest before you're dumped.

29. A wise investment for a county, state, or nation is buying land to be forever wild.

30. I love a kid who tells me the name of his dog or cat. But my favorite fan letter came from a boy named Charley. After the "Hi Rob," only seven words: "I like your books better than literature."

31. When the war finally ended, in one way or another we all came home wounded. Yet fervently thankful.

32. The basis for my success is that I write about what people *do*. Not what they ought to do.

33. Wish not for apples. Grow strong trees.

# Epilogue

MAY A FEW WEEDS BLOOM IN YOUR GARDEN.

ROB

*Longwood, Florida*
*2005*

# About the Author

ROBERT NEWTON PECK HAS WRITTEN MORE THAN SIXTY-FIVE books, including the highly acclaimed *A Day No Pigs Would Die* and its sequel, *A Part of the Sky*. He is also the winner of the Mark Twain Award for his Soup series of books. Many of his novels are rooted in Vermont farm country, where he grew up, and Florida, his present home.

Rob plays jazz and ragtime piano, and tends eleven mustang horses and two cats. He and his wife, Sam, reside in Longwood, Florida.